A Bible Study for Individuals or Small Groups

JONAH

God's Holy Runaway

Timothy J. Mulder

Copyright © 2025 Timothy J. Mulder

All rights reserved. No part of this book may be used or reproduced by any means, graphic electronic, or mechanical, including photocopying, recording, taping or by any information storage retrieval system without the written permission of the author except in the case of brief quotations embodied in articles and reviews.

This book may be ordered through booksellers or by contacting:

Timothy J. Mulder
www.timothymulder.com
www.armchairtheology.org

Because of the dynamic nature of the Internet, any web addresses or links contained in this book may have changed since publication and may no longer be valid.

Stock imagery © Melissa Askew on Unsplash.

Unless otherwise indicated, scripture quotations are from the ESV Bible®
(The Holy Bible, English Standard Version®)
copyright © 2001 by Crossway Bibles,
a publishing ministry of Good News Publishers.
Used by permission. All rights reserved.

Scripture quotations marked NIV are taken from the Holy
Bible, New International Version®, NIV®.
Copyright © 1973, 1978, 1984 by Biblica, Inc. ™
Used by permission of Zondervan. All rights reserved worldwide.

Credit for the subtitle goes to fourth century theologian, Paulinus of Nola.

Editing assistance by Michelle Mulder, Mike Singenstreu,
and Hannah Feuchtenberger

ISBN: 979-8-9901934-6-8 (p)
ISBN: 979-8-9901934-7-5 (e)

Library of Congress Control Number

Revision date: 09/14/2025

For Rob, the fish that guided me back to dry land.

Table of Contents

Introduction 7

On the Run 17

The Interrogation 31

The Reckoning 43

Jonah's Cry 55

The Narrowing 69

Salvation 83

The Call 97

Repenting 111

Relenting 123

Resenting 135

God's Rebuke 147

God's Response 157

I

Introduction

JEREMIAH 23:19

Behold, the storm of the LORD!
Wrath has gone forth, a whirling tempest;
it will burst upon the head of the wicked.

THE BOOK OF JONAH IS one of the best-known stories in Scripture. If you are at all familiar with the story of Jonah, the image of a fish swallowing Jonah likely leaps to mind. However, the Book of Jonah is not really about the fish. The fish is only mentioned in two verses: when it swallowed Jonah,[1] and when it vomited Jonah out.[2] No other details about the fish are provided. Unfortunately, by focusing on the fish, we miss the greatest miracle in the book – the entire city of Nineveh repenting and turning to the LORD.[3]

---

[1] Jonah 1:17, "Now the LORD provided a huge fish to swallow Jonah, and Jonah was in the belly of the fish three days and three nights."
[2] Jonah 2:10, "And the LORD commanded the fish, and it vomited Jonah onto dry land."
[3] Miles Custis, *Jonah: A Prophet on the Run* (Bellingham: Lexham, 2014), 5.

The Book of Jonah is a short biographical parable about a man who ran from God. While most prophetic books focus on their message, the Book of Jonah focuses on Jonah's story. Despite the book's inclusion with the minor prophets of Scripture, Jonah contains no major prophecies. Jonah's message is incidental.

In this small book,[4] we see God do some amazing things: We see a group of hardened sailors repent and begin new faith in God. We witness Jonah being swallowed by a big fish and surviving for three days. We see the largest city in the world respond to some of the worst evangelism ever. We read about a shade plant blossoming in the desert overnight.

Jonah's story not only follows his physical journey but also his spiritual one. The book focuses on God's relentless pursuit of His self-righteous prophet. While many prophets are models of righteousness, Jonah is not one of them. Throughout Scripture, prophets were typically models of obedience. Not Jonah. He did the exact opposite of what one would expect. When God told him to go east, Jonah went west. When God told him to travel by land to Nineveh, Jonah traveled by boat to Tarshish. When God chose to show mercy to the Gentiles, Jonah did not rejoice – he childishly pouted and evilly wished for their destruction. The purpose of the Book of Jonah can be summarized in four words, "Don't be like Jonah." And yet, we are all like him on a very deep level.

The Book of Jonah does not state who the author is, although a few scholars believe that the author may have been Jonah himself. Jonah was written in the third person, which might indicate that Jonah did not write the book. However, Moses and Isaiah also wrote in third person. If the author was not Jonah, he made some harsh accusations against the man.

Jonah the Prophet
The Book of Jonah is not a parable, but a factual telling of the events of a real person's life. What do we know about Jonah? Jonah's name means "dove" or "pigeon" in Hebrew.[5] Jonah was a prophet to the northern kingdom of Israel.

---

[4] Jonah's four chapters contain just 1368 words in total. (ESV)
[5] In Scripture, the dove often symbolizes the Holy Spirit. This is a fitting name for a prophet, as the Holy Spirit should be evident in every area of his life. After our study of Jonah, perhaps you will agree that his parents might have chosen a different name.

As such, he was an ardent nationalist, pro-Israel and anti-Gentile – or at least anti-Assyrian.[6] Jonah prophesied during the reign of Jeroboam II (782-753 BC) instructing the king to expand Israel's borders. Therefore, the events described in Jonah happened in the eighth century BC. In terms of Hebrew history, this would have been about halfway between the revolt of the northern ten tribes under Jeroboam and their captivity by Assyria in 722 BC.[7] 2 Kings 14:25[8] provides us with a little more information about Jonah. It tells us that he was a prophet from Gath-Hepher, in the territory of Zebulun, about three miles north of Nazareth. The call to Nineveh was not his first assignment. He had been a prophet long before his intimate encounter with the fish.

Jonah's immediate predecessors were Elijah and Elisha. He likely belonged to one of Elisha's schools of prophets. His contemporaries were Amos and Hosea, and he preceded Isaiah. An old Jewish legend maintains that Jonah was the son of the widow of Zarephath, having been raised from the dead by Elijah for future ministry. There may be little or no truth in that. Interestingly, with the exception of Jesus, Jonah is the only Biblical prophet mentioned in the Qur'an.[9] The story of Jonah and the great fish is a favorite topic of Muslim art.

Nineveh

Nineveh was the largest city in the world at that time and diplomatic center of the ancient world.[10] It was Assyria's capital city, and as such, the capital of the Gentile world. Nineveh, from the reign of Shalmaneser I (1273-1274), had been the royal residence of Assyria. It was the largest and most fortified city in the ancient world. According to Hugh Martin, "Profane history reports it as a well-fortified city: "its walls were a hundred feet high, and so broad on the top that three chariots could run abreast, adorned with fifteen hundred

---

[6] Douglas Stuart, *Hosea-Jonah* WBC (Grand Rapids: Zondervan, 1998), 431.
[7] Hugh Martin, *Jonah* Geneva Series of Commentaries (Edinburgh: Banner of Truth, 1995), 1.
[8] 2 Kings 14:23-25, "In the fifteenth year of Amaziah son of Joash king of Judah, Jeroboam son of Jehoash king of Israel became king in Samaria, and he reigned forty-one years. He did evil in the eyes of the LORD and did not turn away from any of the sins of Jeroboam son of Nebat, which he had caused Israel to commit. He was the one who restored the boundaries of Israel from Lebo Hamath to the Dead Sea, in accordance with the word of the LORD, the God of Israel, spoken through His servant Jonah son of Amittai, the prophet from Gath Hepher."
[9] Jack M. Sasson, *Jonah* TAYB (New Haven: Yale, 1990), 159-160. In the Qur'an, Jonah is known as Dhun-Nun (the man of the fish) (21:88) but has also been called "Sahib al-Hut" (Companion of the Fish) in the Qur'an (68:49).
[10] C.F. Keil and F. Delitzsch, *Minor Prophets* Commentary on the Old Testament in Ten Volumes (Grand Rapids: Eerdmans, 1973), 390.

towers, each two hundred feet high."[11] Nineveh was also the base for the Assyrian military. Its war-like culture filled the city with bloodshed and violence.[12] Nineveh was located on the eastern bank of the Tigris River, across from modern-day Mosul[13] (in northern Iraq.) The founder of Nineveh was Nimrod,[14] who was the son of Cush, the grandson of Ham, and the great-grandson of Noah. Hence, Nineveh had been around for 1500 years before Jonah's Mediterranean cruise.

According to Jonah 3:3,[15] Nineveh was so large that it took three days to walk across it. Therefore, if a man can walk 20 miles in a day, that would mean that Nineveh was 60 miles across. However, it is unlikely that any ancient city was that large; after all, the greater Houston metroplex is 52 miles across. How do we explain the size of Nineveh as described in the Book of Jonah? Nineveh was the name of two different things. It was the name of a specific city *and also* the name of a metroplex of five large cities. Nineveh was a city within the greater Nineveh metroplex. Cities in the Nineveh metroplex included Nineveh, Rehoboth, Ir, Calah, and Resen.[16] If we were to measure the size of the area across the greater Nineveh metroplex, it would have been around sixty miles. Additionally, according to Martin, Nineveh "had large gardens and even fields within its walls."[17]

Jonah 4:11[18] explains that Nineveh's population of 120,000 people did not know their right hand from their left. This description has created two primary theories about Nineveh's population. The first theory is that since the

---

[11] Martin, 39.
[12] The Assyrian military and the Ninevites, in particular, were violent. They documented torture methods of captives and displayed dismembered bodies around Nineveh.
[13] Mosul is also filled with bloodshed and violence. Not much has changed in 2800 years.
[14] Genesis 10:8-12, "Cush was the father of Nimrod, who became a mighty warrior on the earth. He was a mighty hunter before the LORD; that is why it is said, "Like Nimrod, a mighty hunter before the LORD." The first centers of his kingdom were Babylon, Uruk, Akkad, and Kalneh, in Shinar. From that land, he went to Assyria, where he built Nineveh, Rehoboth Ir, Calah and Resen, which is between Nineveh and Calah—which is the great city."
[15] Jonah 3:3, "Jonah obeyed the word of the LORD and went to Nineveh. Now Nineveh was a very large city; it took three days to go through it."
[16] Genesis 10:11-12, "From that land he went to Assyria, where he built Nineveh, Rehoboth, Ir, Calah, and Resen, which is between Nineveh and Calah—which is the great city."
[17] Martin, 39.
[18] Jonah 4:11, "And should I not have concern for the great city of Nineveh, in which there are more than a hundred and twenty thousand people who cannot tell their right hand from their left—and also many animals?"

Ninevites did not know the one true God, they wouldn't have known right from wrong, making the population of the city around 120,000. That would mean that Jonah 4:11 was speaking about *all* the Ninevites. The second theory is that Jonah 4:11 is speaking of children, who don't know right from left. Once you add parents and grandparents to that number, the population could be as many as one million. I will use the more conservative figure that Nineveh's population was 120,000.

Despite being the greatest city of the Assyrians, Nineveh was also the most wicked. Over one hundred years later, Nahum would prophesy the destruction of Nineveh.[19] Much of the evil in Nineveh was violence,[20] idolatry, and ignorance of God. Nineveh's wickedness came to the attention of the LORD like that of Sodom and Gomorrah,[21] cities that were infamously destroyed by God when there were not even ten righteous people there.

Says Iain Duguid, "God may indeed be concerned for the evil of the great city of Nineveh, but He is even more concerned about a broken prophet, whose evil also comes before Him. Nineveh's evil was obvious to all and turned out to be surprisingly easy for a sovereign God to heal. Jonah's evil was subtle and deep-rooted: healing him would be a far harder and more delicate task."[22]

Tarshish

We don't know much about Tarshish because its exact location is unknown. Around 1000 BC, Phoenician merchants established trade routes around the Mediterranean Sea. Tarshish was likely the name of one of their settlements. Most scholars agree that Tarshish was the same place as Tartessos, located in southwestern Spain. Tarshish was a mining and smelting center. According to Jeremiah 10:9[23] and Ezekiel 27:12,[24] Tarshish was an important source of silver, iron, tin, and lead. As a result, there were likely plenty of ships sailing

---

[19] All three chapters of the book of Nahum are prophecies against Nineveh.
[20] The Assyrian / Ninevite armies often flayed their enemies alive, cut off their lips, or simply beheaded them.
[21] Genesis 18:20-21, "Then the LORD said, "Because the outcry against Sodom and Gomorrah is great and their sin is very grave, I will go down to see whether they have done altogether according to the outcry that has come to me. And if not, I will know."
[22] Iain Duguid, *The Rebel Prophet: The Gospel in the Book of Jonah* (Glenside: St. Colme's Press, 2022), 9.
[23] Jeremiah 10:9, "Hammered silver is brought from Tarshish and gold from Uphaz."
[24] Ezekiel 27:12, "Tarshish did business with you because of your great wealth of goods; they exchanged silver, iron, tin and lead for your merchandise."

to and from Tarshish.²⁵ It would not have been difficult for Jonah to catch a ride on one. Jonah chose to go to Tarshish to travel as far from Nineveh as possible.

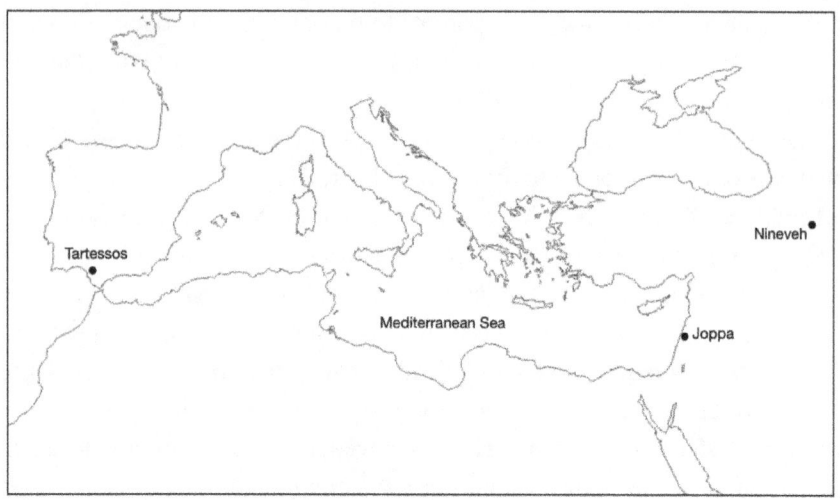

Location of Tarshish and Nineveh

Structure and Themes of the Book of Jonah
The Book of Jonah is four self-contained chapters.²⁶ Jonah's structure is fascinating in that the third and fourth chapters mirror the first and second chapters. Each group of chapters has three sections:
1. God speaks to Jonah (Jonah 1:1 and 3:1).
2. Jonah has an encounter with Gentiles (Jonah 1:4-16 and Jonah 3:1-5).
3. Jonah speaks with God (Jonah 2:1-10 and Jonah 4:1-10).

The Book of Jonah contains three different themes.
1. God allows second chances.²⁷ While God often displays grace and mercy by granting second chances, it is not something He always

---

²⁵ Stuart, 451.
²⁶ They do not rely on any other books to complete the story.
²⁷ 1 John 1:9, "If we confess our sins, He is faithful and just to forgive us our sins and to cleanse us from all unrighteousness."

does. "God is not a harsh parent, but neither is He a soft parent who simply ignores rebellion and wickedness."[28] There are plenty of times in Scripture where He did not give His people a second chance.[29] The Book of Jonah contains three instances of God affording people second chances. "It is pretty clear in the Bible story that the whale swallowing Jonah wasn't meant as a punishment from God. It was God saving him from drowning. So, it was actually provision to give him a second chance. The whale itself was the start of Jonah's second chance."[30]

2. God brings life from death. This is one of the central themes of the Bible. Luke 15 tells us the story of the prodigal son, who in his father's words, "was dead, and is alive again; he was lost and is found."[31] There are countless other times in Scripture where the dead are brought to life. John 12:24 tells us, "Truly, truly, I say to you, unless a grain of wheat falls into the earth and dies, it remains alone; but if it dies, it bears much fruit." Removing the stain of sin and restoring life from death culminated with the resurrection of Jesus Christ, who conquered death and is alive at the right hand of God the Father. God is in the business of bringing life from death. It's what He does. It's who He is.

3. Salvation belongs to the LORD.[32] At the end of Jonah 2, Jonah declares that salvation belongs to the LORD. Salvation does not belong to man. Nor does it belong to man and God. It is solely the business of God. This is great news for all of us! It means that we cannot do anything to earn our salvation. From beginning to end, the responsibility for salvation belongs to God alone. Therefore, if salvation belongs to God, there is nothing we can do to lose our salvation either. Since salvation belongs to the LORD, we can rest in the knowledge that He holds us firmly in His grip and will never let us go.

---

[28] Duguid, 36.
[29] In 1 Kings 13:11-25, God allows a lion to kill the prophet who disobeyed Him. In Leviticus 10, God killed Nadab and Abihu when they offered an unauthorized sacrifice to the LORD. In 2 Samuel 6, Uzzah was killed for touching the Ark of the Covenant.
[30] Phil Vischer, director. *Jonah: A Veggie Tales Movie. Behind the Scenes: Jonah and the Bible.* Big Idea Entertainment, 2002.
[31] Luke 15:24, "'For this my son was dead, and is alive again; he was lost and is found.' And they began to celebrate."
[32] Jonah 2:9, "But I with the voice of thanksgiving will sacrifice to you; what I have vowed I will pay. Salvation belongs to the LORD!"

The Book of Jonah also displays missional truths:
1. God calls His people to seek the repentance of the nations. We are to share the Gospel with others to bring about repentance and change in their lives. God calls us to do so in the Great Commission.[33] Anytime people repent, God is praised. [34]
2. God's people will suffer divine displeasure if they fail to extend God's mercy to the nations. The Great Commission is not optional. It is a command and must be followed accordingly.
3. God delights in showing mercy to repentant Gentiles. One of the purposes of the Book of Jonah was to show Israel that God loves nations other than Israel.[35] To Jonah's dismay, one of those nations was Assyria. These truths apply to people from other countries and also to those with different ideologies than ours. Since God loves people from other nations and cultures, we must share the Gospel with all, regardless of race, gender, religion, political stance, or belief system. This is the very thing Jonah did not want to do.

At its heart, the Book of Jonah is about fulling the Great Commission. Does God love people from all cultures? Jay Sklar said, "Do we really believe this to be true? Do we believe that God loves those in Muslim nations? Hindu nations? Buddhist nations? Do we speak of people from these nations as though they really bear God's image and need His grace? Or do our thoughts and words and deeds betray a different attitude?"[36] We do not get to play God and decide whom His chosen people are. That decision was made before the creation of the earth. Therefore, we must not be like Jonah in the manner in which we interact with those from other cultures or belief systems. All of

---

[33] Matthew 28:18-20, "And Jesus came and said to them, "All authority in heaven and on earth has been given to me. Go therefore and make disciples of all nations, baptizing them in the name of the Father and of the Son and of the Holy Spirit, teaching them to observe all that I have commanded you. And behold, I am with you always, to the end of the age."

[34] Luke 15:7, "Just so, I tell you, there will be more joy in heaven over one sinner who repents than over ninety-nine righteous persons who need no repentance."

[35] It also subtly compared Nineveh to Israel, who never repented with the sincerity that Nineveh did.

[36] Sklar, 420.

mankind has been created in God's image, and therefore must be shown grace, mercy, and love. Even if our culture says that they are lesser than us, or worse, our enemies.

If we chose to run from God's Great Commission in our lives, we may be surprised at the lengths God will go to get us back on track. So, if you find yourself undergoing an unpleasant journey in nauseating circumstances, this book may help you reflect on how you got there, and where God is taking you. Additionally, since Jonah is only four chapters long, I encourage you to read through it before beginning this study.[37]

---

[37] This introductory chapter is 2½ times longer than the entire Book of Jonah.

1

On the Run

JONAH 1:1-6

Now the word of the LORD came to Jonah the son of Amittai, saying, ² *"Arise, go to Nineveh, that great city, and call out against it, for their evil has come up before me."* ³ *But Jonah rose to flee to Tarshish from the presence of the LORD. He went down to Joppa and found a ship going to Tarshish. So, he paid the fare and went down into it, to go with them to Tarshish, away from the presence of the LORD.* ⁴ *But the LORD hurled a great wind upon the sea, and there was a mighty tempest on the sea, so that the ship threatened to break up.* ⁵ *Then the mariners were afraid, and each cried out to his god. And they hurled the cargo that was in the ship into the sea to lighten it for them. But Jonah had gone down into the inner part of the ship and had lain down and was fast asleep.* ⁶ *So the captain came and said to him, "What do you mean, you sleeper? Arise, call out to your god! Perhaps the god will give a thought to us, that we may not perish.*

AFTER READING ABOUT JONAH'S DISOBEDIENCE, one cannot help but wonder why God would call Jonah to go to Nineveh, instead of one of his contemporaries, such as Amos or Hosea. Nineveh was the largest city in the world. God probably should have sent a prophet who was on his A-game. However, from God's perspective, Jonah was the right man for the job. He was a seasoned prophet, preaching to Northern Israel for most of his life. Who better to send to another nation than a man with experience? God decided to send a seasoned veteran to Nineveh, for this was an important mission.

Jonah was accustomed to being rejected by those to whom he proclaimed God's Word. After all, he had likely warned Israel to repent and return to the LORD. From Jonah's perspective, prophesying was terrible enough in unrepentant Israel. If Israel hadn't heeded his warnings, why would Nineveh do so? Jonah disobeyed God's call to go to Ninevah and he showed no compassion to the Ninevites. But God knew the Ninevites would repent while Israel continued to harden their hearts.

Jonah's Disobedience

God's call to Jonah required immediate submission. There should have been no questions, comments, or delays. Jonah was a mouthpiece for God and he did as he was told. Most of the time. He had a personal relationship with God. However, he engaged in a course of disobedience that would take him across the known world and away from God's presence. The narrator emphasized Jonah's rebellion by mentioning three times that Jonah was headed to Tarshish, which was in the opposite direction as Nineveh. (See map in Introduction.)

Not only did Jonah disobey God, but he deliberately went in the other direction. (Nineveh lay to the east; the Mediterranean Sea and Tarshish were to the west.) Because Jonah disagreed with God's call to Nineveh, he did the opposite of what he was told. In doing so, Jonah displayed a fundamental mistrust of God. He doubted God's sovereignty and His love for Gentiles, even Ninevah. By attempting to flee, Jonah tried to get to a place where no fellow believers could be found. This is evident in the choice of Joppa as the departing port. The majority of the dock workers there were Gentiles. Additionally, those who sailed ships out of Joppa were almost always Phoenicians. And Tarshish was a place where there were likely few if any,

Israelites. It sounds like a paradise for a prophet on the run. The means of Jonah's disobedience appeared at the docks of Joppa. William Banks says, "When a person decides to run from the LORD, Satan always provides complete transportation facilities."[1] "The sinner will usually find the implements and opportunities which a heart set to do evil will easily transform into sin."[2] Jonah found that the events to help him disobey lined up perfectly. And he pounced on the opportunity and headed down to Joppa.

Prophets were not to *flee from* God's presence. They were to *stand in* God's presence.[3] Surely, Jonah knew that he could not flee from God. It is laughable that he tried to in the first place. According to Gregory of Nazianzus, "To imagine that Jonah hoped to hide himself at sea and escape by his flight the great eye of God is utterly absurd."[4] Nineteenth-century Scottish minister Hugh Martin says, "The wicked, indeed, habitually act as if God were not omnipresent." Jonah knew that God was omnipresent,[5] but sometimes sin robs us of the truths we know. So, Jonah boarded a ship for Tarshish in a pointless effort to flee from God's presence. He may have run from God, but God didn't have to run to catch him.

The question then arises, "Is it possible not to be in God's presence?" Genesis 4:16[6] tells us that Cain *went out from God's presence*. 2 Kings 13:22-23[7] tells us that God *would not cast Israel from His presence*. In Jeremiah 23:39,[8] God tells false prophets that He *will cast them from His presence*. The difference between Jonah attempting to flee from God and these passages is that only God is able to ban people from His presence. Voluntarily leaving God's presence is not something that mortal man may accomplish on his own. Like Jonah, we cannot escape His presence, no matter how far we run or how

---

[1] William Banks, *The Reluctant Prophet* (Chicago, Moody, 1966), 20. While this is meant to be humorous, God provided the boat to bring Jonah back to Himself.
[2] Martin, 60.
[3] Jay Sklar, *Jonah* ESVEC (Wheaton: Crossway, 2018), 399.
[4] Gregory of Nazianzus, *Jonah* ACCS, Volume XIV: The Twelve Prophets (Downers Grove: IVP, 1993), 133.
[5] Omnipresent means that God is present everywhere simultaneously.
[6] Genesis 4:16, "Then Cain went away *from the presence of the* LORD and settled in the land of Nod, east of Eden." (italics added)
[7] 2 Kings 13:22-23, "Now Hazael king of Syria oppressed Israel all the days of Jehoahaz. But the LORD was gracious to them and had compassion on them, and He turned toward them, because of His covenant with Abraham, Isaac, and Jacob, and would not destroy them, nor has He *cast them from His presence* until now." (italics added)
[8] Jeremiah 23:39, "Behold, I will surely lift you up and *cast you away from my presence*, you and the city that I gave to you and your fathers." (italics added)

hard we try. Jonah knew this, being familiar with Psalm 139:7-12, which reads,

> Where shall I go from your Spirit? Or where shall I flee from your presence? If I ascend to heaven, you are there! If I make my bed in Sheol, you are there! If I take the wings of the morning and dwell in the uttermost parts of the sea, even there your hand shall lead me, and your right hand shall hold me. If I say, "Surely the darkness shall cover me, and the light about me be night," even the darkness is not dark to you; the night is bright as the day, for darkness is as light with you.

Did Jonah run because he was fearful for his life? After all, sending an Israelite to preach in 8th century Nineveh would be like sending a Jew to preach in Berlin in the 1930s.[9] He would be one man surrounded by tens of thousands of his mortal enemies as he prophesied their destruction. Sure, prophets did this all the time - *in Israel*, where they had reasonable assurance that no one would kill God's prophet. But in Nineveh, all bets were off. Jonah may have been legitimately afraid. Wouldn't we be afraid? I might be willing to be a street preacher in Las Vegas. But if God wanted me to do so in Iraq, I might act like Jonah and board a ship for Tahiti.

Many of us have had times when we were unsure of what God wanted us to do. Jonah, on the other hand, had no excuse. God's directions in verse 2 were clear: "Arise, go to Nineveh, that great city, and call out against it, for their evil has come up before me." God commanded Jonah to denounce the evil in Nineveh. It was "a sudden, abrupt summons to duty."[10] Jonah could not say he didn't understand the call. There were no explanations or additional details necessary. Sinclair Ferguson says, "Our problem in obeying God is not that we do not understand what He is saying, but that we do!"[11] Jonah's difficulty was not confusion, but that his desires were not God's desires. What about us? Do we trust the LORD to be God, even when He asks us to do something that makes no sense to us – even if it sickens us to think of doing

---

[9] Ferguson, 51.
[10] Martin, 26.
[11] Sinclair Ferguson, *Man Overboard! The Story of Jonah* (Edinburgh: Banner of Truth, 2018), 12.

what He tells us to do? If we are not willing to trust God when He doesn't act the way we think He should, then we are not really trusting Him. We may act like Christians, but in our hearts, we have no relationship with Him.[12]

Hebrew Nationalism
There must have been a solid reason why Jonah, a faithful prophet of the LORD, would suddenly decide to no longer obey God's call in his life. Leslie Allen calls Jonah "intensely patriotic, a highly partisan nationalist."[13] Having lived his entire life among the ten tribes of the Northern Kingdom, Jonah reasonably assumed he would spend the rest of his life there. After all, God had limited His revelations to the Israelites for many years. The attitude amongst the Hebrews of Jonah's day was that God revealed Himself *only* to Israel. It was the conclusion of the Jews that all Gentiles were under the curse of spiritual death. Jonah struggled to believe that God would save the pagan Ninevites.

Had the Assyrians made repeated covenants with the God of the Hebrews? Did God lead the Assyrians out of Egyptian captivity and through the Red Sea on dry ground? The Assyrians were most certainly not God's chosen people. They were lowly Gentiles. In Jonah's mind, they were filthy dogs! And everyone except God, apparently, knew that Hebrews and Gentiles don't mix. Hugh Martin said that the Jews, "had forgotten that the covenant with Abraham, Isaac, and Jacob embraced the Gentile world very specially in its gracious primeval provisions: 'In thy seed shall all the nations of the earth be blessed.'"[14] Jonah did not want to denounce evil in Nineveh because he did not want them to repent. The best way to keep Nineveh from repenting was to not go in the first place.

Another of Jonah's issues with the call to Nineveh was that Nineveh was an enemy of Israel. Israel, at the time, had been paying tribute to Assyria and had been doing so since the reign of King Jehu (842-815 BC).[15] Jonah could not believe that God would send him there. As we shall see in the final chapter of the book, Jonah would rather die than see God be gracious and merciful to

---

[12] Duguid, 16.
[13] Leslie Allen, *The Books of Joel, Obadiah, Jonah, and Micah* (Grand Rapids: Eerdmans, 1976), 202.
[14] Martin, 4. See also Genesis 22:18, "And in your offspring shall all the nations of the earth be blessed, because you have obeyed my voice."
[15] In 722, Assyria would invade Israel.

Israel's enemies. Douglas Stuart said, "Jonah wanted no part of something as horrible as mercy shown to a brutal, oppressing, enemy nation."[16]

> Jeremiah sought the honor of God and the honor of Israel.
> Elijah sought the honor of God and not the honor of Israel.
> Jonah sought the honor of Israel, and not the honor of God.
>
> *Adapted from Mekilta, Pisha*

While there can be no doubt that Hebrew nationalism played a part in Jonah's motivation to flee from the face of God, that is not the reason given in Scripture. Later in the book, we are provided with insight into Jonah's mindset when he fled. Jonah 4:2 tells us that Jonah "prayed to the LORD and said, 'O LORD, is not this what I said when I was yet in my country? That is why I made haste to flee to Tarshish; for I knew that you are a gracious God and merciful, slow to anger and abounding in steadfast love, and relenting from disaster.'" Jonah rationalized that God would relent in bringing disaster to Nineveh. Jonah's true problem was not with the Ninevites but with God. Jonah ran from God because he knew that God would show mercy, and he had no desire to see Nineveh repent.

The Resulting Storm
Says Ferguson, "The ship lying in the Joppa harbor was not meant to be a means of escape from God's clearly revealed word, but the most terrible instrument in the hands of God to bring His servant back to his senses."[17] God "hurled a great wind upon the sea." The words of verse 4 leave no doubt that God was behind the storm.[18] God's hand in the storm was recognized, even by the Gentile sailors, who were Phoenicians from different locations and

---

[16] Stuart, 453.
[17] Ferguson, 21.
[18] Jonah 1:4, "But the LORD *hurled* a great wind upon the sea, and there was a mighty tempest on the sea, so that the ship threatened to break up." (italics added)

worshiped different gods. The divine storm was sent to pursue, arrest, and punish Jonah.[19] The storm was an expression of God's displeasure, but also a conduit through which God pursued Jonah. And yet, simultaneously, it threatened the lives of others on the sea.

The storm had three effects on the seasoned sailors. 1. These usually brave and bold men were frightened. 2. Each man cried out to his god.[20] The sailors took a shotgun approach to requesting God's assistance: they prayed to every god they could think of in hopes that one of them would be the correct god and would grant their request. 3. As a last resort, the sailors threw their cargo overboard to lighten the load.

Jettisoning the cargo was a last-ditch effort to save their lives. However, their efforts were not enough. Chrysostom said this, "They threw overboard the wares that were in the ship into the sea; but the ship was not getting any lighter, because the entire cargo still remained with it, the body of the prophet, the heavy cargo, not according to the nature of the body, but from the weight of sin. Nothing is so heavy and onerous to bear as sin and disobedience."[21]

This was no regular storm; it was on the verge of destroying the ship. God has the powers of nature in His hand and uses those powers to accomplish His purposes. The Bible does not say that every difficulty is the result of sin – but it does teach that every sin will bring you into great difficulty.[22] And Jonah's sin of running away from God brought him into intense difficulty.

What about the sailors? Was it fair that their lives were endangered because of Jonah's sin? It doesn't seem fair for God to threaten their lives because of the sin of another. But there is precedence of God doing just that. In Joshua 7 because of Achan's sin, 36 Israelite soldiers died in the battle with Ai. Additionally, once Achan was found guilty, his entire family, and all their animals were killed with him. What about King David in 2 Samuel 24? David took a census that God did not authorize, and because of his sin, 70,000 Israelites died. Was it fair that so many died because of Achan's and David's disobedience?

God's justice does not always seem *fair* to our limited human perspective. But, we are fine with it when His justice results in mercy: one man died so that countless others might live. Jesus Christ died on the cross to pay the price

---

[19] Martin, 73.
[20] Deep down, all men know God exists. Reason tells us this. However, that knowledge is insufficient to establish a relationship with Him. And reason alone does not lead us to God.
[21] Chrysostom, *Jonah* ACCS, Volume XIV: The Twelve Prophets (Downers Grove: IVP, 1993), 132.
[22] Tim Keller, *The Prodigal Prophet* (New York: Penguin Random House, 2018), 24.

of sin so that many would have eternal life. That may not be *fair*, but we happily accept the result. Ultimately, God's authority in meting out His justice is absolute. And in this case, God worked through this life-threatening storm to bring the sailors, not to death, but to a saving faith.

Sleeping on the Job

When the sailors went into the ship's hold to retrieve the cargo, they found Jonah fast asleep.[23] Jonah had likely fallen asleep before the storm began, and as a result, was oblivious to the panic above him. The sailors immediately informed the ship's captain that Jonah was sleeping in the hold. Since Jonah worshiped a different God than the rest of the men on the ship, the captain figured Jonah's God might be the one who could calm the storm. The captain approached Jonah and reproved him for being selfish and unconcerned with the well-being of the other sailors, saying "What do you mean, you sleeper? Arise, call out to your god! Perhaps the god will give a thought to us, that we may not perish."[24] The captain showed that he had some faith – he knew that the lives of the sailors were at the mercy of the hand of God.

The captain's words "arise" and "call out" are the same words God used to command Jonah to go to Nineveh just a few days earlier. As a prophet of God, one of Jonah's roles was to intercede with God on behalf of others. By sleeping in the cargo hold, Jonah avoided that responsibility. Jonah, a follower of the living God, was rightfully rebuked by a Gentile. He deserved it. He was not displaying trust in God. He was not bearing testimony to those around him. As Christians, we don't like to be rebuked by the world, but sometimes, the world's rebuke is justified and necessary. God can use the rebukes of a Gentile to correct a sinner.

---

[23] There are multiple similarities between this part of Jonah and the story of Jesus calming the storm in Mark 4:37-38. "And a great windstorm arose, and the waves were breaking into the boat, so that the boat was already filling. [38] But He was in the stern, asleep on the cushion. And they woke Him and said to Him, "Teacher, do you not care that we are perishing?" Jonah 1:6, "So the captain came and said to him, "What do you mean, you sleeper? Arise, call out to your god! Perhaps the god will give a thought to us, that we may not perish."
[24] Jonah 1:6

Don't Be Like Jonah
It is interesting that Jonah did nothing until he was rebuked. The sailors, who were convinced they would die as a result of this storm, repented and were converted to faith in the true God. Jonah never repented, sought forgiveness or displayed any concern or empathy for his fellow sailors.

One of the missional truths of the Book of Jonah is that God cares about how we relate to those who are different than us. Jonah wanted to work for the good of the Jews. He disobeyed God's call to go to Nineveh and was silent when the Gentile sailors on the boat were crying out for help. Jonah hadn't wanted to preach repentance to Gentiles, but on the boat to Tarshish, he found himself talking to them about God. Now, amid a storm from God, Jonah could no longer hear God's call to witness to Nineveh. Instead, all he could hear was the rain and thunder surrounding him. The storm preached the omnipotence of God better than Jonah could have hoped to do. After all, nothing is secure when God is against it.[25]

We are to be respectful toward those who are different than we are. Jonah found it deeply disturbing that God was asking him to sacrifice his reputation by preaching repentance to Gentiles – and for the sake of the Ninevites, these 'Gentile dogs' who "deserved neither mercy nor grace from God or Jonah!"[26] Jonah wanted "a God of his own making, a God who simply smites the bad people, for instance, the wicked Ninevites, and blesses the good people, for instance, Jonah and his countrymen."[27] In this aspect, we are not to be like Jonah. We are to care deeply for those who are different than we are.[28]

We all run from God. Every one of us has made a conscious decision to turn from God and disobey Him at some point in our lives. For some of us, we have fled the love of God and sought after the idols of our choosing. Like the prodigal son, we find ourselves living in the lowest, filthiest sin we could ever imagine. But you can "never outrun God or escape His perfect will for your life. Indeed, when you have run as far as you can, you will find that He has run further and is waiting there to greet you and show you the grace that you have long resisted to welcome you into His safe harbor in Christ."[29] Tim

---

[25] Jerome, *Jonah* ACCS, Volume XIV: The Twelve Prophets (Downers Grove: IVP, 1993), 132.
[26] Ferguson, 14.
[27] Keller, 5.
[28] Matthew 22:36-40, "Teacher, which is the great commandment in the Law?" And He said to him, "You shall love the LORD your God with all your heart and with all your soul and with all your mind. This is the great and first commandment. And a second is like it: You shall love your neighbor as yourself. On these two commandments depend all the Law and the Prophets."
[29] Duguid, 21.

Keller says "The gospel is this: we are more sinful and flawed in ourselves that we ever dared believe, yet at the very same time, we are more loved and accepted in Jesus Christ than we ever dared hope."[30] As a prophet, Jonah ran away from God, but we have a Prophet who was perfectly obedient for our sake.[31] He did not rebel but rather placed His Father's will before His own. In the place of the runaway prophet, God sent a Prophet to redeem the runaways. Stop running from Him and rest in the reality of His love.

---

[30] Timothy Keller and Kathy Keller, *The Meaning of Marriage: Facing the Complexities of Commitment with the Wisdom of God* (New York: Penguin Publishing Group, 2013), 44.

[31] Matthew 5:17-20, "Do not think that I have come to abolish the Law or the Prophets; I have not come to abolish them but to fulfill them. For truly, I say to you, until heaven and earth pass away, not an iota, not a dot, will pass from the Law until all is accomplished. Therefore, whoever relaxes one of the least of these commandments and teaches others to do the same will be called least in the kingdom of heaven, but whoever does them and teaches them will be called great in the kingdom of heaven. For I tell you, unless your righteousness exceeds that of the scribes and Pharisees, you will never enter the kingdom of heaven."

Chapter 1 Discussion Questions

1. Have you ever tried to escape or hide from God's presence? If so why?

2. What does God's pursuit of Jonah tell us about His pursuit of us?

3. Why do you suppose that Jonah was calm and able to sleep during the storm while the sailors were afraid for their lives?

4. Compare and contrast Jonah on the ship in the storm in Jonah 1 and Jesus calming the storm in Mark 4:35-41.

5. Interpret the following passages in light of God's command to preach to the Ninevites:
   • Matthew 15:21-28

   • Matthew 22:1-14

- Matthew 28:18-20

6. Has this chapter revealed to you that there are peoples to which you are not passionate about sharing the gospel? If so, whom?

- How can you change your attitude?

- How can you support those who are passionate to reach them?

2

The Interrogation

JONAH 1:7-10

And they said to one another, "Come, let us cast lots, that we may know on whose account this evil has come upon us." So, they cast lots, and the lot fell on Jonah. ⁸ Then they said to him, "Tell us on whose account this evil has come upon us. What is your occupation? And where do you come from? What is your country? And of what people are you?" ⁹ And he said to them, "I am a Hebrew, and I fear the LORD, the God of heaven, who made the sea and the dry land." ¹⁰ Then the men were exceedingly afraid and said to him, "What is this that you have done!" For the men knew that he was fleeing from the presence of the LORD because he had told them.

NOW THAT THE CAPTAIN HAD roused Jonah from his nap in the cargo hold, the sailors set about to determine who among them was the cause of the great storm. Since no one confessed to being responsible for the storm, the sailors cast lots to determine guilt. Once the guilty party was selected, they began to interrogate him. While the Hebrew states that the sailors "said" to Jonah, "Tell us on whose account this evil has come upon us," I think it is more likely that the sailors used stronger language. I find it hard to believe that they just had an ordinary, sit-down chat about what Jonah had done. I suspect it was more of a hurried interrogation. An interrogation is a type of interview frequently used by law enforcement agencies or military organizations with a single objective: to elicit helpful information quickly. After all, they were at sea amid a terrible storm. I am sure their conversation was aggressive and abrupt. The sailors needed to ascertain the cause of the storm.

Casting Lots
The idea of deciding something by casting lots may appear superstitious to modern minds. However, it is more common than you might think. In the movie *No Country for Old Men*, Anton Chigurh flips a coin to determine whether he will kill the person he's talking to. To him, the coin represents the randomness and risk of every moment of human life. When the gas station clerk asks him what he's risking in calling the coin toss, Chigurh answers, "You've been putting it up your entire life. You just didn't know it." When we think the coin symbolizes randomness, Chigurh turns around and suggests that the coin has some predetermined fate attached to it: "You know the date on this coin? . . . 1958. It's been traveling for 22 years to get here. And now it's here, and it's either heads or tails."[1] The casting of lots can be used in one of two ways. Lots can be used innocently when they are used to decide something that men cannot make an unbiased choice about. For example, lots are cast (a coin is flipped) at the beginning of a football game to determine who gets the ball first. Lots can also be used with negative intent when they are used for personal gain, such as gambling.

Casting lots was a practice used to decipher God's will. Because the outcome produced by casting lots was random, the result was seen as divine. This practice was used not only in Israel but in other ancient nations as well. Scripture does not tell us that the Hebrews used dice for lots, and nations around them used bones, stones, sun-dried and fired clay, shafts of arrows,

---

[1] *No Country for Old Men*, directed by Ethan Coen and Joel Coen, (Los Angeles, CA. Paramount Vantage, 2007), mp4.

and sticks of wood.² Therefore, it is likely that the Hebrews also used these means. Scholars suggest that the casting of lots commonly involved two dice, each with three black sides and three white sides. The dice were rolled, and if two black sides came up, the answer was to the negative. Two white sides indicated positive. One black and one white side meant the dice needed to be rolled again.

The principle implied in the casting of lots is that a request is made of God to indicate His divine direction. Typically, the casting of lots was accompanied by prayers asking God to control the outcome. The sailors cast lots because no one among them, including Jonah, was willing to confess. Someone was holding out. Since nobody came forward to accept responsibility for the storm, they had no choice. The sailors relied on the casting of lots to discover that Jonah was the guilty party.

While Hebrew law forbade fortune-telling, the casting of lots was an acceptable practice. There are several instances in Scripture of the casting of lots. In 1 Samuel 10:20-21,³ Samuel cast lots to determine the first king of Israel. The lot fell on Saul, son of Kish. In Acts 1:26,⁴ the remaining eleven disciples cast lots to determine who would take the place of Judas. The lot fell upon Matthias. In John 19:23-24,⁵ the Roman soldiers at Jesus' crucifixion cast lots for his tunic.

Instances where the casting of lots were used to discover a guilty party are found in 1 Samuel 14 and Joshua 7. In 1 Samuel 14:42,⁶ lots were cast to see who had broken King Saul's foolish vow of fasting. The lot fell upon his son, Jonathan, the guilty party. But of all the Biblical references to the casting of lots, Joshua 7:16-18⁷ is the most similar to Jonah 1:7. In Joshua 7, Israel

---

² Sasson, 109.
³ 1 Samuel 10:20-21, "Then Samuel brought all the tribes of Israel near, and the tribe of Benjamin was taken by lot. He brought the tribe of Benjamin nearby its clans, and the clan of the Matrites was taken by lot; and Saul the son of Kish was taken by lot. But when they sought him, he could not be found."
⁴ Acts 1:26, "And they cast lots for them, and the lot fell on Matthias, and he was numbered with the eleven apostles."
⁵ John 19:23-24, "When the soldiers had crucified Jesus, they took His garments and divided them into four parts, one part for each soldier; also, His tunic. But the tunic was seamless, woven in one piece from top to bottom, ²⁴ so they said to one another, "Let us not tear it, but *cast lots* for it to see whose it shall be." This was to fulfill the Scripture which says, "They divided my garments among them, and for my clothing they *cast lots*." (italics added)
⁶ 1 Samuel 14:42, "Then Saul said, 'Cast the lot between me and my son Jonathan.' And Jonathan was taken."
⁷ Joshua 7:16-18, "So Joshua rose early in the morning and brought Israel near tribe by tribe, and the tribe of Judah was taken. And he brought near the clans of Judah, and the clan of the Zerahites was taken. And he brought near the clan of the Zerahites man by man, and Zabdi

was fresh off the victory at Jericho. The next city on their radar was Ai. Since Ai was a much smaller city than Jericho, Israel only sent 3,000 troops into battle. They were soundly defeated, with thirty-six soldiers dying in battle. The LORD directed Joshua to cast lots to find out whose sin caused the disaster. The lot fell upon Achan, who had taken spoils from the battle of Jericho. There are five similarities between Jonah 1 and Joshua 7:16-21: 1. Both Jonah and Achan directly disobeyed the LORD. 2. Like Jonah, Achan remained silent during the initial questioning. 3. Both men had to be found out by the casting of lots. 4. They were each questioned before confessing their sins. 5. Both Achan and Jonah only confessed after their sins were exposed! But the most significant difference between Jonah and Achan was that Jonah was a man of God.

Identity

Identity is a popular buzzword today. Because of today's culture, we all have different identities. We have a social identity, religious identity, work identity, national identity, sexual identity, and our true identity. What is interesting is that each of these identities may be different. So, what kinds of things form our identities? Charles Horton Cooley says, "we develop our concept of self by watching how other people react to different versions of ourselves that we present." [8] In other words, our identity is shaped by what others think about us and how they respond to us.

We identify ourselves by multiple factors. How do you introduce yourself at a party? We may identify by our line of employment. Maybe we identify ourselves based on what we believe. Many people try to sculpt their identity by using social media. They project one image when they are something quite the opposite. Commonly we identify by where we are from. For instance, I have lived all of my adult life in Texas. However, I was born and raised in Chicago, so I remain a Chicago Bears fan. I still identify with the city of my youth. Ultimately, each of these identities is a way that others recognize us. Our identities, whether real or crafted, reveal what is important to us.

---

was taken. And he brought near his household man by man, and Achan the son of Carmi, son of Zabdi, son of Zerah, of the tribe of Judah, was taken."

[8] https://www.scribd.com/document/344130037/Charles-Horton-Cooley-pdf. Accessed September 17, 2023.

How we identify with each other can reflect how we identify with God. Many of the things that we identify with have the potential to become idols in our lives. That doesn't immediately make them bad things. For example, my wife and I have twins. For years, we identified as the twins' parents. There is nothing wrong with that. However, perhaps a more important identity for my wife and I is that we are children of God. That identity needs to be the most important in our lives. More important than our occupational, regional, social, political, or even sexual identity.

In verse 8, the sailors ask Jonah four questions to ascertain his identity: They want to know *who* Jonah is. Tim Keller says, "To ask (someone) "Who are you?" is to ask them, "Whose are you?""[9] Our identity's most critical factor is *whose* we are. To whom do you belong? Where does your heart lie? The sailors had likely accepted Jonah's passage on their ship with little or no questions. Now, amidst a hurricane like gale, they wanted to know who he was and why he was there.

The Questioning
In Jonah 1:8, the sailors confronted Jonah, "Tell us on whose account this evil has come upon us. What is your occupation? And where do you come from? What is your country? And of what people are you?" Now that the sailors had identified the guilty party, they began questioning him, hoping they could find out what they should do.

Their first question was, "What is your occupation?" This question can also be translated as "What is your business?" or "What is your trade?" or "What is your mission?" Their purpose in asking about Jonah's line of employment was two-fold: 1. They were trying to find out if he was involved in a disreputable occupation, which may have brought about the wrath of the gods. 2. They were trying to determine if his occupation was tied to a specific deity so they could know which god Jonah had upset. In the ancient Near East, different jobs had different gods.

Jonah's occupation was a prophet. His mission was to preach repentance to the biggest city in the world. But he didn't tell them that. The sailors' first question confronted Jonah with the reality of his disobedience and betrayal of his occupation.

The sailors' next three questions were of a similar vein, "Where do you come from?" and "What is your country?" and "Who are your people?" In the

---
[9] Keller, *Prodigal,* 49.

Bible, someone's *country* was a large part of their identity. Knowing Jonah's occupation would be helpful to a degree, but if the sailors were going to find out specifically which god was angry enough to send a storm, they needed to know the national god of the guilty party. As we will see in a moment, Jonah stated that he was a Hebrew which implied that he worshiped Israel's national God, Yahweh. Asking Jonah where he was from would help them identify the offended god a little faster.

Jonah's Answers

Jonah had fallen greatly, was pursued hotly, and was disciplined by the LORD Almighty with a firm hand of chastisement. Now, he had to answer for his offenses. Jonah's answers show us that God was slowly drawing him closer to repentance.

It is important for a moment to address the topic of repentance. Repentance is an active two-step process: turning *away* from sin and turning *toward* God. The first part of repentance, the turning away from sin, includes confessing sins to God and asking His forgiveness. The second part, the turning toward God, includes not repeating that sin and reconciling to God. When confronted after committing adultery with Bathsheba and having her husband, Uriah, murdered, David, in Psalm 51:1-2,[10] provides an excellent example of a prayer of repentance. The Psalm reflects David's genuine desire for true reconciliation with God. This is what made David a man after God's own heart. Like all imperfect humans, he failed at times. What set David apart was that he earnestly sought and experienced forgiveness and restoration of communion with God. Ultimately, David loved God and sought to follow His law. The primary difference between David and Jonah is that nowhere, in his actions or words, did Jonah repent. His heart was still hard. This was reflected by the fact that he did not confess until after he was chosen by lot, and when questioned, he was less than truthful with his answers.

---

[10] Psalm 51:1-2, "Have mercy on me, O God, according to your steadfast love; according to your abundant mercy, blot out my transgressions. Wash me thoroughly from my iniquity and cleanse me from my sin!"

Upon reading verse 9, you may have noticed that Jonah didn't answer the questions in the order they were asked.[11] Instead, he answered the questions in order of importance to him. Jonah answered the questions about his nationality first. He gave them the key part of his identity. "I am a Hebrew." Jonah was proud that he hailed from God's chosen people. His heritage was what Jonah felt was most important. However, this answer was of almost no value to the sailors. In the ancient Near East, people had three types of gods: personal, family, and national. By saying he was a Hebrew, Jonah avoided discussing his personal faith in God, opting to discuss the national God of Israel instead. Discussing a national god is less personal than revealing details about one's relationship with that god. In saying this, Jonah distanced himself from his sin.

Jonah then discussed the national God that his countrymen worshiped. But, due to the order in which he responded, we know that the God he worshiped was not as important to Jonah as his national identity. Despite saying he feared the LORD, Jonah's actions indicate that his faith was not as deep as we would expect from a man of God. His faith is shallow.[12] Genuine fear of the LORD results in unwavering obedience. This was the opposite of what Jonah did. His claim to fear the LORD was simply not true. However, by saying God's name, Yahweh (translated as the LORD), Jonah provided the sailors with the name of the deity who caused the storm. Jonah further clarified the God he spoke of, calling Him "the God of Heaven." In the ancient Near East, calling a god the God of Heaven indicated that He was the supreme being. Jonah then took it further and said that his God created the sea and the dry land.[13]

Regarding his occupation, Jonah never stated that he was a prophet. He conveniently left that detail out of his answers. Perhaps, because he was running from God, he was unsure that he was a prophet any longer. While Jonah was being confronted with his sin, three things were occurring:

1. The sailors were afraid. Initially, they were terrified of the storm. Now that they knew that God was wronged, they were afraid of the LORD. The author of Jonah, in saying that the sailors *"feared with great fear*, means that they were so smitten, that they perceived that

---

[11] Jonah 1:9, "And he said to them, "I am a Hebrew, and I fear the LORD, the God of heaven, who made the sea and the dry land."
[12] As we will see in the next chapter, while Jonah's fear of the LORD was shallow, the sailors' fear of the LORD was deep and genuine.
[13] Later in the story, Jonah's God commands the sea and dry land to bring about His will.

the God of Israel was a righteous judge, and that He was not such as other nations fancied Him to be, but that He was capable of affording dreadful examples whenever He intended to execute His vengeance."[14]

2. Jonah was forced to admit what he had done to earn God's wrath. The result of the lots, the omnipresence of Jonah's God, and Jonah's explanation caused the sailors to ask Jonah the ultimate question, "What is this that you have done?" They were not asking Jonah about the nature of his sin but rather exclaiming the horror of his attempted flight from the LORD. And now, the pagan sailors rebuked the prophet of the LORD. They could not believe that Jonah had chosen their ship to attempt to escape his sovereign LORD.

3. God has not relented in His punishment of Jonah. Jonah's confession was not enough to satisfy God's wrath; there had to be consequences.

We need to notice in this exchange, that Jonah showed little or no concern for the Gentile sailors. He exhibited no empathy or regret for their terror or the peril he had brought upon them. His heart did not appear to be softening. Jonah may have decided that the sailors were excluded from the Kingdom of God and, as such, were not worth saving. How often are we guilty of this? How many times do we lack compassion or fail to witness to others because we have pre-judged them based on their identity?

Judging others is not our role in God's kingdom. Our role is to "make disciples of all nations, baptizing them in the name of the Father and of the Son and of the Holy Spirit, teaching them to observe all that Jesus has commanded us."[15] The key word in this verse is "all." We are not to discriminate against countries we don't like when we share the Gospel or support missions. Now, there is nothing wrong about feeling passionate about missions to a certain country or people. In fact, the Holy Spirit may be

---

[14] Calvin, *Commentaries,* Volume 14. (Grand Rapids: Baker, 1993), 53.
[15] Matthew 28:18-20, "And Jesus came and said to them, "All authority in heaven and on earth has been given to me. Go therefore and make disciples of *all* nations, baptizing them in the name of the Father and of the Son and of the Holy Spirit, teaching them to observe all that I have commanded you. And behold, I am with you always, to the end of the age." (italics added)

drawing your heart to a specific area for a reason. But this does not excuse neglecting missions to countries or peoples because we don't like them.

Christianity is growing faster in atheist Communist China and in Muslim African nations than it is in the United States. This is because others set aside their bias and sometimes personal safety to go and tell as Jesus instructed. We need to actively root out the sin of discrimination in our hearts. This goes beyond national civil rights or social trends to accept others' differences. To fulfill the great commission, we must love others as Jesus did and that means that we cannot limit who we support or witness to, based on their country, ethnicity or even the religion of their nation. To do otherwise is to callously shrug our shoulders while they sink beneath the waves.

Chapter 2 Discussion Questions

1. Whose are you? What factors influence your identity? What do you need to change to become more Christ-like?

2. Did Jonah fear God as he claimed? Do his actions confirm that?

3. As we see in Jonah's story, God uses suffering to convict us of our sins. Has God brought about suffering due to sin in your life? What did that look like?

4. How we respond to suffering and fear indicates the condition of our hearts. How have you responded to these things in your life? What needs to change for you to respond better?

5. Read John 4:16-26. How were the Samaritan woman's answers to Jesus' questions similar to Jonah's answers about his personal relationship with God?

6. Read Luke 10:25-37. How was Jesus challenging His listeners with the national identities of those in His parable?

3

The Reckoning

JONAH 1:11-17

Then they said to him, "What shall we do to you, that the sea may quiet down for us?" For the sea grew more and more tempestuous. ^{12} He said to them, "Pick me up and hurl me into the sea; then the sea will quiet down for you, for I know it is because of me that this great tempest has come upon you." ^{13} Nevertheless, the men rowed hard to get back to dry land, but they could not, for the sea grew more and more tempestuous against them. ^{14} Therefore, they called out to the LORD, "O LORD, let us not perish for this man's life, and lay not on us innocent blood, for you, O LORD, have done as it pleased you." ^{15} So they picked up Jonah and hurled him into the sea, and the sea ceased from its raging. ^{16} Then the men feared the LORD exceedingly, and they offered a sacrifice to the LORD and made vows. ^{17} And the LORD appointed a great fish to swallow up Jonah. And Jonah was in the belly of the fish for three days and three nights.

UP UNTIL NOW, JONAH'S CONDUCT had been despicable. He had been self-centered, caring only about himself, and disobeying the LORD'S command to witness to the Ninevites. He was apathetic toward the sailors, sleeping during their greatest hour of need. All parties understood that it was Jonah's sin that had caused the storm. Jonah confessed his sin against God, and yet the storm had not let up and the ship was about to break apart. Because Jonah did not fully repent, the storm did not relent. However, beginning with verse 12, his behavior toward the sailors became noble and worthy of admiration. It seems as though Jonah may have finally accepted the consequences of his rebellion.

Jonah's Instructions

Despite jettisoning the cargo, anxious prayers, and a hurried interrogation revealing Jonah's sin, the sea continued to rage. Jonah was responsible for the storm and the expert on how to calm it. He alone knew what it would take for the LORD to relent in His anger. Now, it was a matter of Jonah's rebellious will fighting against God's perfect will. Hurling cargo overboard bought the sailors more time, but it did not remove them from danger. At some point, Jonah was going to have to repent.

Jonah's comment in Jonah 1:12, "Pick me up and hurl me into the sea; then the sea will quiet down for you, for I know it is because of me that this great tempest has come upon you," shows that he accepted his fate. He realized the depth of his sin and knew what he must do to stem the tide of consequences caused by his rebellion. He exhibited a calm dignity towards the sailors.[1] As a believing Hebrew, Jonah was well acquainted with the justice of his holy God. Based on the Scriptures and Israel's experience as a nation of God's chosen people, Jonah knew that God's justice was often swift and severe. By instructing the sailors to hurl him into the sea, Jonah was telling them the only way to satisfy God's demand for justice. He alone had to answer for his rebellion. His instructions to the sailors indicated that he had acknowledged God's actions were just. However, confession and true repentance are not the same thing. Jonah's confession does not mean that he repented

---

[1] Martin, 173.

Repentance is a two-step process. It requires a turning away from sin and turning toward God. Confessing one's sins is only half of the equation. The other half of repentance is reconciliation, which is turning toward God in faith. It involves realigning one's will to that of the LORD. Jonah had confessed his sin and calmly accepted the consequences. But accepting the consequences and resigning oneself to punishment is not the same as repentance. God must occupy the place in your heart where sin once resided.[2]

Restitution is a common theme with the modern criminal justice system and recovery support groups. It involves recognizing how your actions have hurt others, accepting the consequences, and taking steps to make things right. Jonah's request to be thrown overboard could be seen to be restitution, but repentance is about the heart, and Jonah's heart was still running away. Jonah's rebellious flight was no match for God's sovereignty. Despite rebelling against God, deep down Jonah feared Him. And so it is: Jonah became the judge in his own case.[3]

That being said, the question then arises as to whether Jonah's statement in verse 12 demonstrates selflessness or stubbornness on Jonah's part. Selflessness in that Jonah was willing to die so the sailors might live. Stubbornness that in dying, Jonah would not have to go to Nineveh. Did he finally love his fellow man so much that he was ready to die for them? Or would he rather die than obey God's command? Timmer said, "His choice to go overboard rather than repent shows that he would rather die than change course."[4] Jonah would rather face death than participate in anything that might be for the good of Nineveh. He was willing to die to spare the lives of the mariners, but participating in the salvation of Nineveh was too much.

Notice that at no time in the first chapter did Jonah use language of repentance. We don't know if he experienced a change of heart, but none is mentioned. However, we can see by his actions that he was willing to sacrifice himself for the mariners. Jonah, in the last part of verse 12,[5] shows that he was taking responsibility for the calamity that he had brought upon the

---

[2] Matthew 12:43-45, "When the unclean spirit has gone out of a person, it passes through waterless places seeking rest but finds none. ⁴⁴ Then it says, 'I will return to my house from which I came.' And when it comes, it finds the house empty, swept, and put in order. ⁴⁵ Then it goes and brings with it seven other spirits more evil than itself, and they enter and dwell there, and the last state of that person is worse than the first. So also, will it be with this evil generation."
[3] Martin, 177.
[4] Daniel Timmer, *A Gracious and Compassionate God* (Downers Grove: IVP, 2011), 71-72.
[5] Jonah 1:12b, "I know it is because of me that this great tempest has come upon you."

mariners, not because he was looking at God, but because he was looking at the sailors. And this is significant because it shows his lack of true repentance.

The Sailors' Attempt to Save Jonah

Throughout the Old Testament, we are shown that sin requires a sacrifice to be forgiven by God. Starting in the Garden of Eden, animals were slain after Adam and Eve sinned. God killed an animal to cover Adam and Eve's nakedness and shame after they ate the forbidden fruit. This established the precedent of shedding blood to provide for the forgiveness of sins. Under Mosaic law,[6] God required His people to sacrifice animals for atonement. The priests were to shed the blood of perfect animals, including bulls, goats, and doves, for the sins of God's people. But the Old Testament sacrifices were never enough to fully remove the stain of sin from the souls of men.[7] A perfect sacrifice was needed. All Old Testament sacrifices point forward to ultimate sacrifice of the Lamb of God. This is why Jesus Christ became man and sacrificed Himself for the sins of His chosen people. Christ's perfect sacrifice was sufficient to establish the forgiveness of sins for all time.

Though the sailors had confronted Jonah about his sin, they did not condemn him. They showed him grace and attempted to spare his life by getting to shore.[8] They were trying to escape the storm and save the lives of all involved. They forgot about their danger and tried to save their fellow man.[9] They showed Jonah far more compassion than he had shown them. Verse 13 tells us that "the men rowed hard to get back to dry land, but they could not." No. They could not. They were fighting against the LORD's storm. The more they rowed, the harder the storm blew. Their efforts were not enough to thwart the will of the God of Heaven.

Why were the sailors resistant to throw Jonah overboard? Why did they work so hard and continue to risk their lives when the prophet of the LORD

---

[6] Leviticus 17:11, "For the life of the flesh is in the blood, and I have given it for you on the altar to make atonement for your souls, for it is the blood that makes atonement by the life."
[7] Hebrews 10:11, "And every priest stands daily at his service, offering repeatedly the same sacrifices, which can never take away sins."
[8] It may not have been far. Mariners usually sailed within sight of land for navigation. Their salvation may have been tantalizingly within view.
[9] Even those unfamiliar with boats know it is not wise to bring a boat to shore during a storm because it may be dashed upon the rocks.

had offered a simple solution? Is this really surprising? A key plot twist in modern action movies is that the older, wise person offers to sacrifice themselves for the salvation of the group. And yet the group will fight against this solution, sometimes putting themselves at further risk. For our sailors, there were two possible reasons:

1. Even though they were Gentiles, they valued human life. Murder is condemned in most cultures, regardless of religious beliefs. The mariners may also have been familiar with Genesis 9:6, "Whoever sheds the blood of man, by man shall his blood be shed, for God made man in His own image."
2. The sailors witnessed the wrath of God firsthand by the hurricane-like storm. They likely did not want to anger God further by killing His prophet. They did not want God's wrath turned upon them. They did not want to disobey the LORD and bring judgment on themselves. Therefore, they did nothing rash to provoke God's anger. They were already afraid of perishing in the storm. Now, they feared perishing from killing the LORD'S prophet.

Jonah's Sacrifice

According to Sinclair Ferguson, "Jonah's ears heard no longer the word of God or the voice of conscience, but the angry tones of nature, the storms and tempests of heaven, accusing him of guilt."[10] And now all parties involved realized Jonah's time had come. With their hearts in the right place, these seasoned sailors knew they must take a human life. There was no other option. They had tried to avoid this situation but were no match for God's will. According to Hugh Martin, it was as if the sailors cried out to God, "We beseech Thee, O LORD, we beseech Thee, let us not perish for this man's life, and lay not upon us innocent blood: for Thou O LORD, hast done as it pleased Thee."[11] The sailors obeyed God's decree and did nothing on their own direction. Nor did they cast blame for their actions on God. They did what Jonah refused to do.

Notice that the text does not say that Jonah dove into the sea. He had the sailors hurl him into the sea instead. This indicates Jonah's refusal to act on his own accord to save the lives of the sailors. He was still hesitant! However, in asking to be thrown overboard, Jonah demonstrated some degree of empathy for the sailors. God was using the events of the storm to bring about

---

[10] Ferguson, 24.
[11] Martin, 184.

a love for humanity in Jonah's heart. He was teaching Jonah that repentant Gentiles were not enemies of Israel. Whether or not that would sink into Jonah's hardened heart remained to be seen. Jerome says that Jonah "did not refuse, prevaricate, or deny; but having made confession concerning his flight, he willingly endured the punishment, desiring to perish, and not let others perish on his account."[12]

Jonah's storm was a matter of life and death. From the sailors' perspective, Jonah was going to die once they threw him overboard. However, Jonah's storm was about much more than the wind, the waves, and the ship breaking apart. Jonah's storm was worse than a physical storm – it was spiritual. Jonah's storm raged inside of him. He was drowning not in water but in God's anger. This internal storm was a matter of rebellion or submission, defiance or obedience, death or life. There can be no greater storm in a man's life than clashing his will against God's. Man will always have inner turmoil until he submits to God's will. Until Jonah submitted to God's will, he would continue to experience turmoil far worse than what he experienced in the wind and rain.

The Sailors' Actions

The author's use of the word hurled in verses 4, 5, and 15 is interesting. The repeated use of the word indicates emphasis. In verse 4, the LORD "hurled" the wind into the sea, thus causing the great storm. In verse 5, the sailors "hurled" the cargo into the sea in their attempt to live. In verse 15, the sailors, also in their effort to live, "hurled" Jonah into the sea. To hurl something means "to throw it with great force" or "to push someone violently." This is precisely what the sailors did when they threw Jonah overboard: they used great force. They did not pick up Jonah and gently toss him into the sea. They violently shoved him overboard. There was no gentleness in their actions. The sailors had been pushed to their limits by the storm and the ethical dilemma of killing Jonah. Their response was a hurried and anguished one, done forcefully so they could put the entire situation behind them.

Though the sailors had failed to save Jonah, their actions displayed the state of their hearts. It showed their respect for human life, their hesitancy to

---

[12] Jerome, 134.

shed blood, and their heroic willingness to give their lives to save another. These were good men of integrity. And God pursued their hearts and souls to achieve His divine purpose. God's storm changed the eternal destiny of each man involved. God's purpose for the storm was not only to elicit a repentant and contrite heart from Jonah, but also to secure salvation for the Gentile sailors. However, their actions thus far did not satisfy God's demand for justice. All sin demands a sacrifice. And Jonah's sin was no different.

The sailors then prayed to God (though Jonah did not) and asked God's mercy as they prepared to throw Jonah overboard. God had made His verdict against Jonah, and the mariners were merely the executioners. The drowning of Jonah would not be their fault. No guilt would rest on them.

So, they picked Jonah up and hurled him into the sea. The moment Jonah hit the water; the storm ceased. Scripture doesn't say that it slowly calmed down. The waves didn't go from tempest to choppy to rough to calm. As soon as Jonah entered the water, it was calm. Verse 15 tells us that "the sea ceased from its raging." To rage is to show violent, uncontrollable anger. The seas went from violent and uncontrollable to immediately calm and tranquil. If the sailors needed any more proof that the storm was God's doing, the sudden calming of the sea proved it. The immediate cessation of the storm showed that the raging seas were solely the result of Jonah's sin, and the sailors had not shed innocent blood by sacrificing him. God has the power to start and stop a storm. And as He stopped it, the sailors' fear of Him grew exponentially.

Verse 16 tells us three things that happened due to throwing Jonah into the sea: 1. The sailors feared the LORD. 2. The sailors made sacrifices to the LORD. 3. The sailors made vows to the LORD. These actions showed the depth of the sailors' conversion. It was genuine. If they had doubted that God was the force behind the storm, they did so no longer. God called the sailors to Himself, and unbeknownst to Jonah, they now trusted in the LORD for their salvation. We know theirs was not a "foxhole conversion," as the mariners worshiped God after the storm. Their understanding of God had expanded beyond Jonah's understanding. They now knew the one true God. Gentiles had once again been brought into the Kingdom of God. And this was precisely the reason behind Jonah's rebellion in the first place! Despite his efforts to keep Gentiles from the Kingdom of God, Jonah had failed, and in his failure, ushered them into God's Kingdom. Says Daniel Timmer, "Jonah's antimissionary activity ironically resulted in the conversion of non-Israelites."[13] The sailors were "utterly transformed by their encounter with Jonah, and especially with Jonah's God. The change in their hearts would be one that would last for the rest of their lives. What had happened to the sailors was the most shocking and incredible experience of their lives."[14]

Jonah's heart, however, was less affected.[15] The ship in the Joppa harbor was not meant to serve as an instrument of escape for Jonah but rather a means of bringing Gentile sailors to salvation. God used Jonah regardless of the condition of his heart in that his flight was not without spiritual fruit. God uses us for His glory, even when our hearts are not aligned with His. We *will be* His witnesses. The question is, "What kind of witnesses will we be?"

The Aftermath
The thunder and the lightning vanished. The clouds dissipated. The ship held together. The storm abated as though it had never happened. But the sailors were changed men. And as all fishermen love to recant the tale of a great storm, they undoubtedly went on to share their story of God's salvation in ports up and down the Mediterranean, resulting in even more souls being ushered into God's Kingdom. If this had been the end for Jonah, they would have honored his sacrifice for the rest of their lives with testimony about the mighty power and mercy of Israel's God.

Jonah still feared God. He had offended Him and attempted to flee from Him, but he still feared Him and had been willing to accept God's judgment for his foolish actions. However, it was not God's desire to merely disgrace Jonah. Jonah needed to have his vision of God expanded, even after all the years of serving Him. God needed to teach Jonah about disobedience. But after learning that lesson, Jonah would still have to call out to the Ninevites.

Before Jonah even hit the water, the God he disobeyed was in the process of saving him. Beneath the water's placid surface, God had prepared deliverance for His prophet. In one of Scripture's best cliffhanger verses, we read that the LORD appointed a great fish to swallow Jonah. Maybe the sailors even witnessed the incredible sight as the fish breached the water to carry

---

[13] Timmer, 77.
[14] Stuart, 465.
[15] Duguid, 13.

Jonah back to the depths. "Beneath the surface, God carried on the marvelous story, more marvelously still, bringing in His own unique, peculiar work of – life in the midst of death."[16] God brought life from death, victory from loss, and glory from doom. God was working out His sovereign will for all to see. In Genesis 18:14,[17] God asked Abraham, "Is anything too hard for the LORD?" The response then, the response in the story of Jonah, and the response today is still a resounding "No!" God's will cannot be thwarted. And so, not expecting the power of God to save him, Jonah found himself, not only still alive, but in a most peculiar situation.

---

[16] Martin, 186.
[17] Genesis 18:14, "Is anything too hard for the LORD? At the appointed time I will return to you, about this time next year, and Sarah shall have a son."

Chapter 3 Discussion Questions

1. What were the sailors afraid of? How did their fear transform from worldly fear to godly fear? What is the difference?

2. The sailors on the ship suffered because of the storm but came out of the ordeal with a healthy fear of God. Have you gone through suffering that wound up being used for your good? If so, when?

3. What was Jonah's motivation for having the mariners throw him into the sea? Was his sacrifice selfless or not?

4. Jonah asked the sailors to throw him overboard to die, but God had a fish waiting to save him. What encouragement can we take from verse 17?

5. How do the sailors show true repentance to the Lord? What actions did they take to demonstrate the sincerity of their repentance?

6. What is the difference between confession, restitution and repentance? What about Jonah's words and actions conveyed confession and restitution but not repentance?

7. Jonah's conflict with God's will was greater than the physical storm he was experiencing. Have you experienced internal storms? How did your will conflict with God's will? How did your defiance turn out?

8. Nowhere in Jonah 1 did Jonah ask for God's help. Have you ever avoided asking God to help you? If so, when and why?

4

Jonah's Cry

JONAH 1:17-2:3

*And the L*ORD *appointed a great fish to swallow up Jonah. And Jonah was in the belly of the fish three days and three nights.* [1] *Then Jonah prayed to the L*ORD *his God from the belly of the fish, saying,*

[2] *"I called out to the L*ORD*, out of my distress,*
    and He answered me;
out of the belly of Sheol I cried,
    and you heard my voice.
[3] *For you cast me into the deep,*
    into the heart of the seas,
    and the flood surrounded me;
all your waves and your billows
    passed over me.

SPOILER ALERT: JONAH DOES NOT die. Although the story doesn't end with Jonah 1:16, it could. The story would be complete. The man of God has been thrown into the sea, resulting in tranquility. The Gentiles have been converted to worshiping the God of Israel. It's a solid ending. However, typical of God, there is another twist in the storyline. God loves to do that. He loves to bring about salvation in unexpected ways. He did so with Samson after his hair was cut and his eyes plucked out. We are told that Samson's hair grew back, and the strength of the LORD returned to him. It was then that he knocked down the temple of Dagon, killing more Philistines with his death than he had during his life. God did so with Jesus, His "illegitimate" Son born to a poor carpenter and his teenage bride in a stable in a small town. No one would have expected that infant to be the Savior of the world, victorious over sin and death forever. God loves to bring about salvation in ways we mortal men would never expect. I suspect it brings Him great joy to see the reactions of men and women when they realize that salvation has come from unforeseen events. Seriously, a great fish? That is how Jonah was saved? I don't think anybody saw that coming. While it comes as a surprise to the reader, it certainly came as a surprise to Jonah!

Then, Jonah 1:17 delivers the cliffhanger verse – the one that leaves us hanging: "And the LORD appointed a great fish to swallow up Jonah. And Jonah was in the belly of the fish three days and three nights."[1] The word "appointed" lets us know that God directed the circumstances to accomplish His will. God is in control; the fish simply obeyed Him. And that brought Jonah to his next location: the "Narrowing." The Narrowing is not death, but it is right there with it. It is an unwelcome lack of comfort. It's the feeling we get when we are caught in a sin. It is what Jonah felt in the belly of the fish.

Jonah 2 begins with Jonah focusing on himself, but by the end, he declares that salvation is from the LORD. In Jonah's prayer, "the one praying for deliverance is more prominent than God the deliverer."[2] It took three days in the belly of the fish before he began praying and offering thanks to God. According to John Calvin, "Jonah, when he was at liberty, became as we have seen, wanton; but now, finding himself restrained by the mighty hand of God,

---

[1] "Three days and three nights" is an ancient figure of speech referring to the amount of time it takes to travel to the netherworld and back.
[2] Timmer, 86.

he receives a new mind and prays from the bowels of the fish."³ It took being in the fish for three days to crack Jonah's hardened heart.

The Fish

Before we dig further into Jonah 2, I want to discuss the elephant in the room. Or, more appropriately, the whale in the tale. The question on everyone's mind is: "What kind of fish was it?" The Greek word used for fish in Jonah 1:17 is *kétos*, which is translated in Matthew as "whale," however, at other times in Scripture, *kétos* refers to other large fish or sea monsters. There are some who argue that the great fish was not likely a whale for two reasons: 1. Whales are scarce in the Mediterranean Sea, especially on the eastern side. 2. Additionally, whales have throats too small to swallow a man whole.

A museum staff member sits inside the jaws of a restored Carcharodon megalodon shark.⁴

---

³ Calvin, *Commentaries,* 74.
⁴ https://digitalcollections.amnh.org/archive/Preparator-Charles-J--Lang-seated-in-Carcharodon-megalodon-jaw-restoration--Fossil-Fish-Hall--Oct--1909-2URM1T1ET0J3.html Accessed July 31, 2025.

Sharks, on the other hand, are frequently found in the Mediterranean, and, if large enough, can swallow a living man whole. Therefore, the fish that swallowed Jonah was most likely a shark. Sharks do not "chew" their food. They bite enough to tear off chunks they can swallow. They frequently swallow items whole, and all manner of items have been found in sharks' stomachs from other large fish to license plates. Secondly, there is archaeological proof that ancient sharks were able to grow much larger than their modern counterparts. The photo of a man inside the jaws of a megalodon skeleton indicates that a large enough shark could have easily swallowed Jonah whole. Jonah 1:17 describes the fish as great, indicating not only that it was of great size, but likely unusually so. Ultimately, it doesn't matter what kind of fish it was. God performed a miracle and preserved Jonah's life by means of that great fish. The fish in Jonah's story fulfilled three roles:

- Savior – the fish was a living life preserver that brought Jonah back to dry land. It was "divine rescue back from the underworld."[5]
- Prison – Jonah was imprisoned in a living, breathing jail, and he could not escape from the fish until God's appointed time of three days and three nights.
- House of Prayer - For Jonah, the fish was a living, breathing house of prayer.

God's Providence
If we were to diagram the first half of Jonah 1:17,[6] we see that God is the subject instead of Jonah. The author did this to show that God orchestrated Jonah's adventure on the sea. From the great storm to a great fish taking Jonah on an unplanned Mediterranean cruise, God providentially cared for the Ninevites by dictating what happened to Jonah. Scripture tells us that all things are controlled by God.[7] Providence means that *all* things are under

---

[5] Stuart, 475.
[6] Jonah 1:17, "And the LORD appointed a great fish to swallow up Jonah. And Jonah was in the belly of the fish three days and three nights."
[7] Romans 8:28, "And we know that for those who love God *all things* work together for good, for those who are called according to His purpose." (italics added)

God's control.[8] This includes a great fish with a belly full of Jonah in the depths of the Mediterranean Sea.

What about things happening by chance? Is there any truth to that? Many of the world's religions believe that most events occur entirely by chance. This is a primary error in the church today. Many evangelicals believe that even the most important things occur completely by chance. Arminianism teaches that the will of man acts without any predetermined certainty. If man acts without any predetermined certainty, how much more does the natural world do so? We must remember that "nothing just happens." There is no such thing as chance. In fact, this concept is a pagan belief. Says Calvin, "Fortune and chance are heathen terms . . . and there is no place in human affairs for fortune and chance."[9] God sent the fish to save Jonah from certain death by drowning. But the fish also served God's greater purpose of saving the city of Nineveh.

By sending the fish to save Jonah, God showed Jonah that he didn't have a choice whether or not to obey his call to go to Nineveh. Yahweh was in control. The fish did what it was commanded to do. And God was going to win this power struggle with His holy runaway. For the time being, Jonah was in the dark, inside something that had swallowed him and kept him from drowning.[10] But let us dispel the mental picture of Jonah kneeling in saintly prayer in the belly of the beast. The stomach likely gripped tight around him, awash with stomach acid, and filled with partially digested fish. With no light to see, only a sulphureous pocket of air to breathe, and a caustic miasma sloshing around him, Jonah was alone with no choice but to consider what God called him to do. He had nothing else to do but ponder his sin and what God would do with him next.

Glimmers of Hope

Since his not-so-bright decision to run from God, Jonah felt the pain of divine opposition. Hugh Martin asks, "Is not this the very trial of faith; namely, to have circumstances to contend with which appear to extinguish hope, yea, which viewed in themselves, not only appear to but actually do shut out all

---

[8] Matthew 10:29-31, "Are not two sparrows sold for a penny? And not one of them will fall to the ground apart from your Father. But even the hairs of your head are all numbered. Fear not, therefore; you are of more value than many sparrows."
[9] John Calvin, *Institutes of the Christian Religion* Book 1, Chapter 16, Section 8 (Grand Rapids: Eerdmans, 1981), 169.
[10] Stuart, 469.

hope whatsoever?"[11] In this dark and dreadful place, at the lowest of depths, in the bowels of the ocean, in the most hopeless of situations, Jonah experiences glimmers of hope. In the place where there is no light, Jonah has the light of faith.[12]

Common sense would mandate that he was in despair However, he overcame common sense with faith in his God's promises. Here, we have a conflict between common sense and faith. Consider many of Jesus' miracles. Common sense would say that the lame would never walk, the leper would never be made clean, and the blind would never see. However, when Christ healed them, He told them, "Your faith has healed you."[13] Faith in Holy God always trumps common sense.

In the fish, Jonah was a captive audience with no choice but to call out to God. Note how verse 1[14] calls God "his God." Jonah still had a relationship with God. He maintained that the LORD was his God. That had not changed. And as long as that relationship existed, Jonah had hope. God, in His redeeming love, began reaching through this low point in Jonah's life and started the healing process of his heart. God used these events to bring Jonah to this exact point. Jonah's afflictions had driven him back to God. Back from unbelief, Jonah's faith returned afresh – more ready to obey than before. It is the same with us. We often begin to witness God's involvement in our lives when we are at our lowest. When we are at this point, we must pray in faith. What else, other than the prayer of faith, can sustain us in these situations? Jesus, in John 6:37, promises that "whoever comes to me I will never cast out."[15] When we are at our lowest point, we must turn to Jesus, for He will not cast us out. We know God is there in the difficult times, but when we see His light break through the clouds, it is at that point our hearts begin to lift.

---

[11] Martin, 189.
[12] Martin, 203.
[13] Mark 10:52, "Your faith has saved and healed you."
[14] Jonah 2:1, "Then Jonah prayed to the LORD *his* God from the belly of the fish." (italics added)
[15] John 6:37, "All that the Father gives me will come to me, and whoever comes to me I will never cast out."

Jonah's Introspection

Now neck-deep in fish guts, Jonah had the time to think through the past few days' events. In Jonah 1:12, Jonah admitted that the storm was his fault, "He said to them, "Pick me up and hurl me into the sea; then the sea will quiet down for you, for I know it is because of me that this great tempest has come upon you." Jonah 2:3[16] shows us that Jonah understood why he was in his present state. He fully understood that God cast him into the heart of the sea. His current predicament could be nothing but God's judgment upon him. There was no other explanation. Jonah had no doubt who did these things and finally called out to Him.

At the lowest point in his life, Jonah did what the ship's captain told him: "Call out to your God!"[17] Verse 2[18] shows us two things: Firstly, Jonah trusted God enough to pray to Him,[19] although it would be a fair question to ask why he waited so long to do so. Jonah was near death. Jonah said, "Out of the belly[20] of Sheol, I cried." By using the word "belly," the author said that Jonah was deep inside Sheol.

What is Sheol? Fourth-century theologian Theodoret of Cypress translates verse 2 that Jonah went down to the belly of hell. Are hell and Sheol the same thing? Sheol is the Old Testament word for the abode of the dead who are under judgment.[21] When we recite the Apostles' Creed and we say that Jesus descended into hell, we are referring to Sheol, the realm of the dead, not actual hell. According to Matthew Emerson, "Sheol is a place of darkness, but it is also a place where God still remembers His people and where He is still King."[22] Alternatively, rather than dusty graves, sometimes Sheol is equated with the abyss, a place at the bottom of the sea.[23] Jonah was in the

---

[16] Jonah 2:3, "For you cast me into the deep, into the heart of the seas, and the flood surrounded me; all your waves and your billows passed over me."

[17] Jonah 1:6, "So the captain came and said to him, "What do you mean, you sleeper? Arise, call out to your god! Perhaps the god will give a thought to us, that we may not perish."

[18] Jonah 2:2, "I called out to the LORD, out of my distress, and He answered me; out of the belly of Sheol I cried, and you heard my voice."

[19] Interestingly, the word "pray" only appears twice in the Book of Jonah – once in Jonah 2:2 and once in 4:2, which reads, "And he prayed to the LORD and said, "O LORD, is not this what I said when I was yet in my country? That is why I made haste to flee to Tarshish; for I knew that you are a gracious God and merciful, slow to anger and abounding in steadfast love, and relenting from disaster."

[20] The Hebrew word for belly can also be translated as "inner parts."

[21] Psalm 86:13, "For great is your steadfast love toward me; you have delivered my soul from the depths of Sheol." Proverbs 15:24, "The path of life leads upward for the prudent, that he may turn away from Sheol beneath."

[22] https://www.desiringgod.org/articles/what-is-sheol Accessed May 23, 2024

[23] https://www.desiringgod.org/articles/what-is-sheol Accessed May 23, 2024

place of the dead. The fact that Jonah cried out to God from Sheol shows us that we are never too far to cry out to God. Remember that the next time that you are in a situation where God feels distant. Jonah cried from the realm of death and God heard his cries.

Secondly, God was faithful to Jonah's call and responded by answering him. In Mark 11:22-25,[24] Jesus gives us guidelines for prayer, telling us not to doubt but to pray in faith. Additionally, He tells us to forgive others so our heavenly Father may forgive us. Jonah prayed in faith to God. According to verse 4,[25] he believed he would again see God's holy temple. He knew he would live. He knew God would answer his prayers, and indeed, God did. That's what God does; He answers the prayers of those who believe in Him and pray to Him with a childlike faith.

What about Jonah's heart? What was going on there? The status of Jonah's heart is discussed in Jonah 1:17, which tells us that Jonah was in the belly of the fish for three days and three nights *before* he began his prayer. Jonah's prayer was not for deliverance but thanksgiving for the deliverance Jonah had already received. But why did Jonah wait so long to begin praying? Was he not thankful to be saved before the end of three days and three nights? Jonah didn't simply cry out for God to save him, as we are likely to do. Instead, he referred to the Psalms, specifically, psalms of thanksgiving.[26] The topics of these psalms are typically praise for God's protection or deliverance. Deuteronomy 11:18-21 says,

> You shall therefore lay up these words of mine in your heart and in your soul, and you shall bind them as a sign on your hand, and they shall be as frontlets between your eyes. You shall teach them to your children, talking of them when you are sitting in your house, and when you are walking by the

---

[24] Mark 11:22-25, "And Jesus answered them, "Have faith in God. Truly, I say to you, whoever says to this mountain, 'Be taken up and thrown into the sea,' and does not doubt in his heart, but believes that what he says will come to pass, it will be done for him. Therefore, I tell you, whatever you ask in prayer, believe that you have received it, and it will be yours. And whenever you stand praying, forgive, if you have anything against anyone, so that your Father also who is in heaven may forgive you your trespasses."

[25] Jonah 2:4, "Then I said, 'I am driven away from your sight; yet I shall again look upon your holy temple.'"

[26] Examples of psalms of thanksgiving include Psalms 18, 30, 34, 66, 92, 116, 118, and 138.

way, and when you lie down, and when you rise. You shall write them on the doorposts of your house and on your gates, that your days and the days of your children may be multiplied in the land that the LORD swore to your fathers to give them, as long as the heavens are above the earth.

By quoting the Psalms, Jonah practiced Deuteronomy 11. This shows us that Jonah had God's Word written on his heart, so that in the midst of sin and distress, God's Word provided him comfort. What's great about the Psalms is that they are rarely specific about the details of time and place. That way, they are applicable to a variety of circumstances. In quoting the Psalms, Jonah quoted God's Word back to God. Why did he do so? Had God forgotten what He said? No. It's not that God needed to be reminded of what He has said. Jonah did. And we are the same. It is prudent for us to quote God's Word back to Him when we pray as well. When things get difficult in life, we need to turn to the Psalms. No matter what situation you are facing, there is a psalm for that. Studying and memorizing God's Word ensures that the verses written on our hearts will come to mind when we need them. This is what happened as Jonah faced those three dark days. He cried out to God praying psalms of comfort back to Him. Psalms that Jonah expressed in his poem include:

- Psalm 18:5-6, "the cords of Sheol entangled me; the snares of death confronted me. In my distress I called upon the LORD; to my God I cried for help. From His temple He heard my voice, and my cry to Him reached His ears."
- Psalm 30:3, "O LORD, you have brought up my soul from Sheol; you restored me to life from among those who go down to the pit."
- Psalm 42:7, "Deep calls to deep at the roar of your waterfalls; all your breakers and your waves have gone over me."
- Psalm 120:1, "In my distress I called to the LORD, and He answered me."
- Psalm 69:2, "I sink in deep mire, where there is no foothold; I have come into deep waters, and the flood sweeps over me."
- Psalm 88:17, "They surround me like a flood all day long; they close in on me together."

Miracles

The swallowing of Jonah by the fish is difficult for many of us to believe. However, there are more incredible parts of the story. The real miracle is that

Jonah survived in the belly of the fish for three days. This leads no small number of people to question the historicity of the account. How do those who refuse to believe the truth of this account explain what happened?

Many people consider the Book of Jonah to be literary fiction. They maintain that the story of Jonah being swallowed whole and surviving inside the fish for three days is too fantastical and, as such, cannot be historical at all. However, Biblical Greek and Hebrew are more than clear that he was in the belly of an actual, live and breathing fish.

The validity of miracles depends on one's presuppositions. If you believe that miracles never happen, then you cannot believe that Jonah survived three days and three nights in the belly of a great fish. If you believe that miracles can and do happen,[27] then believing this fish story will come easily to you. Miracles are defined as surprising and welcome events that are not explicable by natural or scientific laws and are, therefore, considered to be the work of a divine force. Since miracles defy natural or scientific laws, they are often viewed with skepticism. Miracles are also a question of history and philosophy. If someone rejects a miracle as only a myth because the critic assumes that miracles cannot happen because they are contrary to natural law, that is a philosophical difference. In order to dismiss miracles, the critic will have to reject the possibility of divine intervention. On the other hand, if God is omnipotent (all-powerful), then miracles are possible, and accounts of them cannot be dismissed as myths.[28]

For many of us, it is enough that the story of Jonah is contained in God's inerrant Word. That is all the truth we need. William Jennings Bryant put it well, "If the Bible had said that Jonah swallowed the whale, I would believe

---

[27] Iain Duguid, in his book, *The Rebel Prophet*, says, "And, of course, anyone who confesses the most surprising reality of all-that the infinite God became incarnate in a little baby and then died on a cross for our sins – should have little difficulty with anything else surprising that God does in the Bible." (p 10) If you believe that Jesus was who He said He was, then you should have no problem believing the miracle of Jonah and the whale.

[28] What confounds me is when people are willing to believe that God could cause a miracle but then want to pick that miracle apart to conform with scientific laws and known history of the world. That is why I have to great lengths to describe the plausibility of a large shark swallowing Jonah whole. It might be possible to survive in cramped inhumane conditions without food and water on a small pocket of air for three days. But that does not explain a fish large enough to swallow Jonah whole being there at the exact moment of Jonah's need unless you believe, as the story says, that "God directed it."

it."[29] Literary proof that the author of Jonah believed that this story really happened is found in the fact that there are only two references to the fish: when it swallows and when it vomits. The author does not provide a look at the conditions inside the fish. The author does not embellish the story of the great fish. The author simply tells the story as if he absolutely believes it to be true. And if he believes it, we should too. God's purpose was not Jonah's death. It was Jonah's deliverance—his redemption. God, in His relentless mercy, continued to pursue His holy runaway. Just as God had shown His power over nature by sending the raging seas, God again showed His power over nature by sending a great fish. Throughout the story of Jonah, God showed His power over nature. We see it with the storm and the fish, and we will see God's control of nature again in Jonah 4.

Three Days and Three Nights
Another miracle that we should not overlook is the fact that Jonah remained alive in the belly of the fish for three days and three nights. In ancient Near Eastern mythology, three days and three nights is the length of time it took to travel to the world of the dead.[30] However, it is highly unlikely that this is what the author of Jonah was referring to. He meant for the time frame to be taken literally. John Calvin maintains that Jonah had fallen asleep in the ocean and was awakened by the great fish to further his suffering and bring him to the point of greater repentance. This must have been harder than a hundred deaths.[31] He was not killed but languished in a state somewhere between life and death.

Thus far in our story, Jonah has put himself in a tight spot of his own making. How often do we do the same thing? And then we cry out to God to save us from the tight spot we've gotten ourselves into. What tight spots are you in right now? You are not alone. The Author of your story is there with you in your tight spot. He's been through much worse and will remain at your side while you persevere through the storms of life

---

[29] https://allauthor.com/quote/204846
[30] Landes, G.M. "The Three Days and Three Nights Motif in Jonah," *JBL* 86 (1967), 446-450.
[31] Calvin, *Commentaries,* 71.

Chapter 4 Discussion Questions

1. People seem to really focus on the great fish aspect of the story, even though there are only two verses about it. Why do you suppose that is? Does the great fish merit all the focus that has been placed upon it?

2. Why do you suppose Jonah waited so long in the belly of the fish to start his prayer of thanksgiving?

3. Who in your life has been a "life preserver" and brought you back to dry land?

4. How can knowing God's word and praying it back to Him help in your "tight spots?"

5. Are there any sins for which God has pursued you as He did with Jonah? Give a specific example.

6. Has your heart ever been so hardened by your sins that God had to take drastic steps to break you from them? If so, what did He do?

7. There is no mention of repentance on the part of Jonah. Is there any evidence in Jonah's prayer that he repented of his sins?

8. Does God's providence always bring about our personal happiness? How does Romans 8:28 relate to Jonah's situation?

5

The Narrowing

JONAH 2:4-6

Then I said, 'I am driven away
  from your sight;
yet I shall again look
  upon your holy temple.'
⁵ The waters closed in over me to take my life;
  the deep surrounded me;
weeds were wrapped about my head
⁶   at the roots of the mountains.
I went down to the land
  whose bars closed upon me forever;
yet you brought up my life from the pit,
  O LORD my God.

ONE OF MY SONS IS an electrician apprentice. His job requires him to frequently climb into small spaces, such as attics and crawl spaces that are no more than 2 feet tall. These spaces are often extremely hot and humid or damp and moldy. He comes home covered in dust, dirt, and mud and smells accordingly. I have anxiety just thinking about being in such confining places, but it doesn't bother him at all. This is the exact position in which God placed Jonah – in a narrow, uncomfortable space. Jonah was in "The Narrowing."[1] The Narrowing may be a place of physical confinement, such as a prison cell. Or it may be more psychological or sensory. One example of this is a time-out chair for a small child. The time-out is a restriction of activity and sensory reduction that gives the child time to calm down and think clearly. But in this case, the Narrowing is an uncomfortable place where God places us so that we can deal with our sins. Jonah's Narrowing was inside a fish. In addition to such close quarters, Jonah also had a putrid fish smell. Think about it: Jonah's every breath and gasp were wholly filled with the smell of rotting flesh. That stench permeated Jonah's skin, nose, eyes, and mouth. He could not escape from it. The Ninevites likely smelled him from a few blocks away. There are some who suggest that one of the reasons that they listened to Jonah was because the stomach acids in the fish had begun to eat Jonah's flesh.[2] The Narrowing saturated every area of Jonah's being.

In the Depths
In the Narrowing, Jonah was as close to death as he could be without dying. Before arriving in the belly of the fish, Jonah sank to the depths of the sea. Verses 5-6[3] tell us Jonah experienced the bottom of the ocean and imply that he knew he was going to drown. Four phrases from our text indicate this:
- "The deep surrounded me." Though not likely at the deepest part of the Mediterranean Sea (17,000 feet), Jonah was deep under water, likely near the bottom of the Mediterranean Sea.

---

[1] I am unsure where the term 'Narrowing' came from. It was on a scrap of paper in my Bible and it described Jonah's situation quite well. I'm not sure if I read it in a book or heard it in a sermon, and, while I would like to credit someone with the term, I am unable to find out who it is.

[2] Acid burns the skin and dissolves the fatty tissues which can make the skin slough off. Jonah may have looked and smelled like a rotting corpse.

[3] Jonah 2:5-6, "The waters closed in over me to take my life; the deep surrounded me; weeds were wrapped about my head at the roots of the mountains. I went down to the land whose bars closed upon me forever; yet you brought up my life from the pit, O LORD my God."

- "Weeds were wrapped about my head." While this verse may refer to floating seaweed, it is more likely to refer to other plant life. If Jonah was touching weeds, he must have been near or at the bottom of the sea, where sea grasses grow.
- "At the roots of the mountains." There are steep drop-offs in the eastern Mediterranean Sea that are literally underwater mountain ranges. Jonah was at the base of one of these mountains.
- "I went down to the land whose bars closed around me forever." Jonah was saying that he had no means of escape. Jonah was at the mercy of God.

Throughout his run from God, Jonah was concerned about only one person: Jonah. He displayed this by refusing to witness to the Ninevites. He displayed this by sleeping while the boat was about to capsize. He displayed this by his evasive answers to the sailors' questions. And in Jonah 2:4, the author says Jonah was "driven out." He still wasn't taking responsibility for his actions. He had yet to repent! Daniel Timmer said, "Jonah is glossing over any personal responsibility for his brush with death by affirming the agency of everyone but himself."[4]

But in the belly of the beast, there was no one else to blame. John Calvin said, "It is no little thing to be stripped of self-love."[5] And we can be sure that Jonah was stripped of his self-love in the belly of the fish. Jonah's prayer quoted several Psalms that reflected how he felt about the impossible circumstances in which he found himself:

- Psalm 69:2, "I sink in deep mire, where there is no foothold; I have come into deep waters, and the flood sweeps over me."
- Psalm 5:7, "But I, through the abundance of your steadfast love, will enter your house. I will bow down toward your holy temple in the fear of you."

This displays Jonah's reliance upon God's Word. God's Word was buried deep within Jonah's heart, and when all was stripped from him, nothing could take that away. In verse 4, Jonah said that he would again look upon God's holy temple. Jonah's thoughts turned to the temple, the place of the LORD's presence. God's holy temple was the place where God met with man. It was a symbol of God's presence. By saying that he would look again upon the

---

[4] Timmer, 85.
[5] Calvin, *Commentaries*, 72.

holy temple,[6] Jonah was saying that he was under God's protection and care. He understood he would not die in the fish, but that he would live to be in God's presence again.

What about us? Why do we go through situations like Jonah? God places us in the Narrowing for different reasons. Sometimes, He wants us to deal with the consequences of our sins. It is certainly uncomfortable being caught in sin. Other times, God wants us to renew our faith in Him and acknowledge our dependance upon Him. Tim Keller says, "It is only when you reach the very bottom, when everything falls apart, when all your schemes and resources are broken and exhausted, that you are finally open to learning how to completely depend on God."[7]

God may be teaching us endurance and refining our character. Romans 5:3-5 says, "Not only that, but we rejoice in our sufferings, knowing that suffering produces endurance, and endurance produces character, and character produces hope, and hope does not put us to shame, because God's love has been poured into our hearts through the Holy Spirit who has been given to us." We may never know why God places us in the Narrowing, but regardless, we have to trust Him through it.

In verse 6, the focus of Jonah's prayer shifts from Jonah's soggy predicament to the One saving him from his watery pit. Jonah says, "Yet you brought up my life from the pit, O LORD my God." Only the LORD could do such a thing. And that is wonderful news for many of us who are suffering, whether it be from disease, anxiety, issues at home or at work, or wayward children. Whatever storms have forced us under the waters of life, the LORD will bring up our lives from the pit. However, Jonah's statement was not in the future tense. It was in the past tense. "Yet you *brought* up my life from the pit, O LORD my God." (italics added) Jesus already brought us up from the pit of Sheol. God endured death for us, and if that doesn't communicate His love to you, I don't know what does.

As humans, we tend to ignore God when things are going well, confident in ourselves and our illusion of self-reliance. But the moment things start to go wrong, we bemoan our circumstances and wonder "Why is God doing this

---

[6] Jonah 2:4, "Then I said, 'I am driven away from your sight; yet I shall again look upon your holy temple.'"
[7] Keller, 72.

to me?" Often, we have these little pity parties in our minds, where we think things such as, "God doesn't hear my prayers." Or "God doesn't care about me." Those are lies spread by the enemy. When facing difficulties, it is not our first response to think that it is God expressing His infinite love for us. God loves you. He *died for* you. He died so you could be with Him. So, enough with the lies that He doesn't love or care about you. They are simply not true.

We are often put through periods of suffering for a divine purpose. While God's purpose for the fish may have been punitive for Jonah, the ultimate purpose was to put Jonah back on the right path. Far too often, we must be set back on the right track. And God will use whatever means are necessary to get us there. Sometimes, they are the kind words of a friend, but other times, the storms of life are what is needed to get us where He would have us. Sometimes, they are both.

Some years ago, I struggled with a particular sin in my life. When I made it known to my pastor, he had three options: to be punitive, restorative, or both. We spent many hours discussing my time in the Narrowing and how God used that time to accomplish His perfect will in my life. I can see now how that time and those struggles prepared me in many ways for the ministry I now have. Were it not for the godly love my pastor displayed, I would not be on the course I am. I praise God that my pastor helped me to face the consequences of my sin but, at the same time, worked to restore me to the place of my calling. My pastor was my "great fish."[8]

The Sign of Jonah

Often, when I am speaking with unbelievers about who Jesus is, they will make a statement like, "If only I could see some evidence of Jesus' divinity, then I would believe in Him." What they are saying is that unless they see Him perform a miracle, they will not believe. The scribes and the Pharisees asked Jesus for a sign so that they might believe. When asked for a sign, Jesus

---

[8] See dedication at front of book.

told them the only sign they would receive would be "sign of Jonah." Jesus spoke of the sign of Jonah in Matthew 12:38-42[9] and Luke 11:29-32.[10]

The Jews wanted a sign – something incredible, miraculous, and faith-compelling, something that would force them to believe, something that would make it impossible for them to disbelieve. Jesus provided them with a sign: the sign of Jonah. This meant three things:

1. Jonah was a *type* of Christ. According to Hugh Martin, a type is "an event or ordinance in one sphere, analogous to a corresponding event or ordinance in a higher sphere."[11] For example, in the time of Moses, the bronze serpent[12] was lifted up, and only by looking up to it, God's chosen people be healed. Much in the same way, Christ was lifted up on the cross, and only by looking up to Him can His chosen people be healed. Jesus was speaking about Jonah's warning to evil people. In this matter, Jonah was a type of Christ, while the Ninevites

---

[9] Matthew 12:38-42, "Then some of the scribes and Pharisees answered Him, saying, "Teacher, we wish to see a sign from you." But He answered them, "An evil and adulterous generation seeks for a sign, but no sign will be given to it except the sign of the prophet Jonah. For just as Jonah was three days and three nights in the belly of the great fish, so will the Son of Man be three days and three nights in the heart of the earth. The men of Nineveh will rise up at the judgment with this generation and condemn it, for they repented at the preaching of Jonah, and behold, something greater than Jonah is here. The queen of the South will rise up at the judgment with this generation and condemn it, for she came from the ends of the earth to hear the wisdom of Solomon, and behold, something greater than Solomon is here."

[10] Luke 11:29-32, "When the crowds were increasing, He began to say, "This generation is an evil generation. It seeks for a sign, but no sign will be given to it except the sign of Jonah. For as Jonah became a sign to the people of Nineveh, so will the Son of Man be to this generation. The queen of the South will rise up at the judgment with the men of this generation and condemn them, for she came from the ends of the earth to hear the wisdom of Solomon, and behold, something greater than Solomon is here. The men of Nineveh will rise up at the judgment with this generation and condemn it, for they repented at the preaching of Jonah, and behold, something greater than Jonah is here."

[11] Martin, 313.

[12] Numbers 21:4-9, "From Mount Hor they set out by the way to the Red Sea, to go around the land of Edom. And the people became impatient on the way. ⁵ And the people spoke against God and against Moses, "Why have you brought us up out of Egypt to die in the wilderness? For there is no food and no water, and we loathe this worthless food." ⁶ Then the LORD sent fiery serpents among the people, and they bit the people, so that many people of Israel died. ⁷ And the people came to Moses and said, "We have sinned, for we have spoken against the LORD and against you. Pray to the LORD, that He take away the serpents from us." So, Moses prayed for the people. ⁸ And the LORD said to Moses, "Make a fiery serpent and set it on a pole, and everyone who is bitten, when he sees it, shall live." ⁹ So Moses made a bronze serpent and set it on a pole. And if a serpent bit anyone, he would look at the bronze serpent and live."

represented the Jews of Jesus' day. The thrust of both messages was "repent, for the kingdom of God is at hand." Their messages were of universal judgment, reminding us that all men will stand before their Creator one day. According to Jacques Ellul, "Jonah is not Jesus Christ, but he is one of the long line of types of Jesus, each representing an aspect of what the Son of God will be in totality."[13]

2. Jonah was *similar* to Christ. Jesus never promoted any resemblance between Himself and Jonah. Both Jonah and Jesus were sent to preach repentance. Both displayed self-sacrifice for others. In both cases, God brought life from death, first for the man (Jonah and Jesus) and then for His people. When Christ referred to Jonah's sign, He primarily talked about Jonah spending three days and three nights in Sheol. While Jonah was in the fish for three days, Jesus Christ was in the tomb for three days. There was burial and resurrection in both cases. Because of their sacrifices, Gentiles were welcomed into the Kingdom of God.

3. As Jonah was a *sign* to Nineveh, Christ is a sign to all generations. A sign is evidence needed for someone to have faith, to drive someone from unbelief. The sign of the prophet Jonah was his prophecy of the looming destruction of Nineveh. By telling the Ninevites what would occur if they didn't repent, Jonah provided a sign for them to have faith. The great sign of Christianity is Jesus Christ. Jesus, when offering the "sign of Jonah," was saying that Jonah was the only prophet to reach out to foreigners, outcasts, and the uncircumcised – the very people that Israel hated. The sign is two things:

   - Judgment upon sin - Jonah's sign was also his horrific experience with the fish. This confirmed his message of coming judgment – that God would not allow sin to go unpunished. Christ's sign was His life, death, and resurrection. Christ's death showed that God would not allow sin to go unpunished. While He was sinless, He took on every sin of all of God's chosen people. In return, God's chosen people are spared from the judgment of their sins.
   - God's mercy and love to those who repent. Jonah had been in the belly of Sheol, and yet he was offered salvation. Life was brought from death. Christ's death and resurrection signify the Father's judgment upon sin and His mercy to those who repent. Because

---

[13] Jacques Ellul, *The Judgment of Jonah* (Grand Rapids: Eerdmans, 1971), 36-38.

of Jonah's actions, the Father's judgment against Nineveh has been satisfied. Because of Christ's sacrifice, the Father's judgment against the sins of His chosen people was satisfied for all time.

Keep in mind that there are plenty of differences between Jonah and Jesus. Jonah was guilty and the ship's crew innocent, while Jesus was innocent and the people guilty. Jonah was not only a sacrifice for the lives of the mariners, but he was also punished for his own sin. Jesus died solely for the sins of His chosen people. Jesus did not run from the LORD; He stayed the course, regardless of the pressure on Him, and saved mankind from the storms of sin and death. Jonah fled his call to serve the LORD. Jesus did not. Jonah didn't *really* die. He was mostly dead but was saved by God. God did not punish Jonah nearly as much as he deserved. Jonah had deserted God,[14] and the penalty for desertion is death. In this, a loving God showed grace and mercy to His rebellious prophet. God gave Jonah a second chance.

Jesus really died a physical death. He was declared dead and was buried for three days. Unlike Jonah, who was punished for his own disobedience, Jesus was the sinless, perfect Lamb of God, and took full divine condemnation, so there is none left for those who believe.[15]

One Greater than Jonah

In Matthew 12:38-42 and Luke 11:29-32[16] Jesus said that "something greater than Jonah is here." If we compare Jesus to Jonah, we will find seven different ways in which Jesus is greater.

Jesus is greater than Jonah by the *nature* of who He is. They were both commissioned by God, but that is as far as the similarities of nature can go. Jesus had a perfect, sinless nature. Jonah, as clearly displayed in Jonah 1, did not. Says Hugh Martin, "He that comes from above is above all; he that is of the earth is earthly and speaks of the earth."[17]

---

[14] This is akin to a soldier going AWOL (absent without official leave).
[15] Keller, 65.
[16] See footnotes 9 and 10.
[17] Martin, 298.

Jesus is greater than Jonah by the *office* that he holds. While they both held the office of prophet, Christ was also the High Priest and King. But, regarding the office of prophet, Jesus is the highest, the ultimate prophet. Jesus was greater than Jonah in terms of His commission. Jonah's commission to preach to Nineveh was limited to that specific city, which, even though it had at least 120,000 residents, was nothing compared to all the people in the history of the world. Jesus' commission to preach was for the entire world, for all of God's chosen people in the history of the world.

Jesus is greater than Jonah regarding their *messages*. Jonah's message was limited in scope[18] - not discussing repentance or salvation or the future Messiah. It was fragmentary. His entire message was, "In forty days, Nineveh shall be overthrown."[19] Although there was no call to repentance, the Ninevites repented anyway. Jesus' message was the full Word of God – He is our salvation and our Messiah. He taught and lived out the entire transcript of the Father's will.[20] Jesus' message was, "Repent, for the Kingdom of heaven is at hand!"[21] And yet the Jews did not repent.

Jesus is greater than Jonah in how He *discharges* the office. Jonah was limited to proclaiming what God told him to. Jesus was not. Prophets were not perfect and did sin, as we saw in Jonah 1. The Son of God did not. When God spared Nineveh, Jonah was displeased. When God spared His chosen people, Jesus was pleased. Was Jesus displeased, angry, or disappointed when His message didn't always land on fertile ground? Perhaps, but He knew His message was for the people His Father had given Him.[22] Jesus had the right to be angry when people rejected His message. It was personal to Him. Jonah did not have that right because he was only the messenger.

Jesus is greater than Jonah because He has a greater *right* to call us to repentance. Regarding Jesus' account, He has a claim upon us and a personal right to call His people to repentance. In Psalm 51, David repented before God, saying, "*Against you, you only, have I sinned* and done what is evil in

---

[18] Jonah 3:1-2, "Then the word of the LORD came to Jonah the second time, saying, "Arise, go to Nineveh, that great city, and call out against it *the message that I tell you*." (italics added)
[19] Jonah 3:4, "Jonah began to go into the city, going a day's journey. And he called out, "Yet forty days, and Nineveh shall be overthrown!"
[20] Martin, 301.
[21] Matthew 4:17, "From that time Jesus began to preach, saying, "Repent, for the kingdom of heaven is at hand.""
[22] John 10:27-30, "My sheep hear my voice, and I know them, and they follow me. I give them eternal life, and they will never perish, and no one will snatch them out of my hand. My Father, who has given them to me, is greater than all, and no one is able to snatch them out of the Father's hand. I and the Father are one."

your sight, so that you may be justified in your words and blameless in your judgment." (italics added) Jesus is the representative of the offended Godhead.[23] All sins are sins against God. Therefore, God has a personal right to call His people to repentance. When Christ calls us to repentance, there is no greater call.

Jesus is greater than Jonah because of His *experience* in preaching His message. Jonah was a sign to only the Ninevites. As such, He was a sign of the certainty of the LORD'S vengeance on sin.[24] Jesus was a sign to all generations. Metaphorically, Jonah died and was resurrected. However, he did not die. He was mostly dead,[25] but stopped short of death. Jonah "died" for his own sin. Jesus literally died and was resurrected. Jesus died for the sins of His chosen people, including Jonah.

Jesus is greater than Jonah because He has the *power* to forgive sins. Jonah proclaimed God's wrath, but only Jesus can grant forgiveness. Jonah proclaimed the wages of sin, but Jesus has the power to forgive them.

In the Matthew and Luke texts, Jesus called His generation adulterous. He was not talking about marital infidelity but religious infidelity. "You were a people to your God – bound to Him in a marriage covenant, and the God of Israel, your Maker, was your Husband. You have violated the marriage bond – the covenant of your God."[26] Israel gladly claimed the union with God when it suited them but rejected it when it was inconvenient. But he that rejects Jesus rejects the One who freely offers forgiveness of sins.

Jesus Christ is not only greater than Jonah, but He is also greater than the enemy. The very enemy who introduced sin to mankind back in Genesis 3. Along with those sins came death.[27] One of the themes of the Book of Jonah, and all of Scripture, is that God brings life from death. In His resurrection, Jesus brought life out of sin and death. Therefore, when Jesus said, "Something greater than Jonah is here," we can say, "Something greater than sin and death is here." Christ conquered sin and death so that we might be

---

[23] Martin, 303.
[24] Martin, 305.
[25] To quote the *Princess Bride*, Jonah was "mostly dead."
[26] Martin, 320.
[27] Romans 3:23, "for all have sinned and fall short of the glory of God." Romans 6:23, "For the wages of sin is death, but the free gift of God is eternal life in Christ Jesus our LORD."

forgiven and spend eternity in glory with Him. Praise God! There can be no better news!

Chapter 5 Discussion Questions

1. What is "the Narrowing?" Have you ever experienced it?

2. What are some reasons that God places us in the Narrowing?

3. Do you have any specific psalms memorized to comfort you when you are suffering? If so, which ones?

4. What is the "sign of Jonah" to which Christ refers in Matthew 12:39? Did Christ's answer satisfy the Pharisees' request for a sign?

5. Compare Luke 11:29-32 to Matthew 12:38-41. What is the difference between the "sign of Jonah" in these passages?

6. What does it look like to have hope in the "One who is greater than Jonah?"

7. How does Jonah's story prophecy the story of Jesus?

8. What are some differences between Jesus and Jonah? How do these differences impact your view of Jesus?

6

Salvation

JONAH 2:7-10

*When my life was fainting away, I remembered the LORD,
    and my prayer came to you, into your holy temple.
⁸ Those who pay regard to vain idols forsake their hope of steadfast love.
⁹ But I with the voice of thanksgiving will sacrifice to you;
what I have vowed I will pay. Salvation belongs to the LORD!"
¹⁰ And the LORD spoke to the fish, and it vomited Jonah out upon the dry land."*

IN HER BOOK *A YEAR of Marvellous Ways*, author Sarah Winman, said that "coming back from the dead is not quite the same as coming back to life." While this may be true in some circumstances, it was certainly not for Jonah. Jonah came back to life when he cried out to God from inside the fish. Jonah 2:10 tells us that Jonah got a second chance. Not only had God brought him back from the dead, but God brought him back to life as well. In verses 7-9,

Jonah shifted his focus from self to God. Jonah sought to praise God, and in verses 7-9 he continued praying the Psalms back to God:

- Psalm 143:4, "Therefore my spirit faints within me; my heart within me is appalled."
- Psalm 18:6, "In my distress I called upon the LORD; to my God I cried for help. From His temple He heard my voice, and my cry to Him reached His ears."
- Psalm 3:8a, "Salvation belongs to the LORD!"

It comes naturally to Jonah to quote the Psalms in his prayer to God, and it should come just as naturally to us as well. The only way this will happen is if we immerse ourselves in God's Word. I cannot implore you enough to spend as much time as you are able in His Word!

In verse 7, Jonah is still focusing on himself, as he is described as "fainting away." Fainting implies losing consciousness due to hunger, injury, or exhaustion. But Jonah remembered the LORD and prayed to Him. 1 Thessalonians 5:17 tells us to "pray continually." This is something that Jonah had not done thus far in our story – he had not prayed at all. You would think that a prophet of the LORD spent most of his time praying and studying the Scriptures to be able to hear from God. But Jonah did not seek the LORD until he was at his lowest point – inside a fish at the bottom of the sea. I am reminded of the hymn, What a Friend We Have in Jesus, which contains the lines,

> O, what peace we often forfeit,
> O, what needless pain we bear,
> All because we do not carry
> Everything to God in prayer![1]

How often are we like Jonah and wait until things are at their worst before we pray to the LORD? And yet, that is the opposite of what 1 Thessalonians commands us to do. We are to continually pray. We should be in a continuous conversation with God, not only when things get bad. This would be like a husband who only speaks to his wife when there are problems. Such a relationship would not last very long. A healthy relationship requires constant

---

[1] Joseph Medlicott Scriven, 1855.

communication, regardless of the circumstances. We must communicate with our LORD at all times. We must carry everything to Him in prayer.

One of my pet peeves is when someone says, "Well, I guess the least I can do is pray for you." What??? That is the *least* you can do? That is the *most important* thing you can do! That should be our first line of defense against the evil one. When you are overwhelmed to the point that you cannot do anything but pray, you undervalue your greatest weapon. When someone offers to pray, they are offering to humbly approach the throne of the almighty, sovereign God and seek His help. Our God, who created and flooded the world; the one who blinded Saul and saved Jonah; the God who protected a shepherd boy and slayed a giant. That God! If prayer is sufficient to deal with the most serious problem of all, sin, will not prayer solve every problem in life? It is never too late to turn to our God, who is rich in mercy and love. Jonah was at death's door when he remembered the LORD. It was not too late, as the LORD spoke to the fish and brought Jonah from death to life. As we will see, God restored Jonah, but He would also use him in a mighty way.

Hearing from God

You would think that a prophet of the LORD spent most of his time in prayer and the Scriptures to hear from God. The same is true for us. If we are going to hear from God, the best way is to spend quality time in God's Word and in prayer. What a privilege and a blessing to be able to carry our requests to the throne of God and to read His holy, inspired Word! And yet, many neglect these things every day. We rationalize, "I'm too busy for that," or "I'll get to it later." But, when times of trouble arise, we wonder why we haven't heard from God. Don't tell me you haven't heard from God if you haven't opened your Bible.

Hesed

In verse 8, the word "steadfast love" is used. The Hebrew root word for steadfast love is *hesed*. *Hesed* is one of the key theological concepts of the Bible. *Hesed* appears over 250 times in Scripture, including twice in the Book of Jonah: Jonah 2:8[2] and Jonah 4:2.[3] *Hesed* is not translated by any one English term or phrase. It is a characteristic of God which describes His interactions with His people. *Hesed* conveys the sense of love, faithfulness, kindness, goodness, deep loyalty, mercy, and compassion shown by God. It is how we are to treat others. *Hesed* was best displayed when Jesus came to earth to redeem us.

At its heart, *hesed* is an action. In Jonah, *hesed* is translated as "steadfast love," and implies saving someone in real and desperate need. In Psalm 145:8-9, David described God's *hesed* when he said, "The LORD is gracious and merciful, slow to anger and abounding in steadfast love. The LORD is good to all, and His mercy is over all He has made."

In the Book of Jonah, *hesed* is used to describe how God felt about Nineveh. In Jonah 4:2, Jonah described God as gracious and merciful, slow to anger, and abounding in *hesed*. For Jonah, the concept of *hesed* is directly tied to the identity of God. As a result, Jonah felt *hesed* should only be shown to God's chosen people, the Israelites. Jonah was upset that the LORD would have anything to do with Nineveh, let alone going so far as to show them His *hesed*. But when Jonah prayed in Jonah 2:8, he assumed that since the Ninevites worshiped idols, that they would not experience God's *hesed*.

Praising God

In verse 9, Jonah offered thanksgiving and promised to sacrifice to God. Jonah demonstrated a valuable life lesson: one of the best things we can do in difficult situations is to praise God. When Jonah offered thanksgiving, he was praising God. This turned his focus from himself and his problems to the One who could resolve them. Praising God reorients our focus to Him.

Jonah's prayer in verse 9 is typical of people whom amidst desperate circumstances pray to God and make promises in exchange for His help. Jonah's words were similar to those of the sailors in Jonah 1:16, "Then the

---

[2] Jonah 2:8, "Those who pay regard to vain idols forsake their hope of *steadfast love*." (italics added)

[3] Jonah 4:2, "And he prayed to the LORD and said, "O LORD, is not this what I said when I was yet in my country? That is why I made haste to flee to Tarshish; for I knew that you are a gracious God and merciful, slow to anger and abounding in *steadfast love*, and relenting from disaster." (italics added)

men feared the LORD exceedingly, and they *offered a sacrifice to the LORD and made vows*." (italics added) But as co-heirs with Christ, we are able to boldly approach the throne of God, not in a spirit of fear, but as a son asking his Father. Philippians 4:6-7 says, "Do not be anxious about anything, but *in every situation by prayer and supplication with thanksgiving* let your requests be made known to God. And the peace of God, which surpasses all understanding, will guard your hearts and your minds in Christ Jesus." (italics added) Paul instructed us to pray and be thankful to God in every situation. The confidence to thank God as you pray is not arrogant. It is the gift of peace that guards our minds and hearts that enables us to be thankful even as we make requests. There is no situation that it is too small or exceeds the power of our God. That is why Paul instructed us to pray in *every* situation. For Jonah, every situation would include being inside a fish on the bottom of the Mediterranean Sea.

In verse 9, Jonah declared "Salvation belongs to the LORD."[4] These five words are the key verse of the book, if not in all of Scripture. Jonah ends his prayer as Tim Keller says, "with a shout!"[5] Salvation belongs solely to the LORD. Salvation falls under God's authority only. Man is unable to save himself. "Since salvation is really of the LORD, it can come even to pagan idolaters, turning them into God-fearers just as easily as it can come to people who are very proud of their membership in the covenant community and their correct theology, yet who have hearts that wander far away from the LORD."[6] Jonah has gone from focusing on himself to the message he was initially called to proclaim. His physical and spiritual salvation belonged to the LORD. "No other words could summarize better Jonah's appreciation for all God has done for him."[7] Paulinus of Nola said, "Hoping for salvation by human resources is no salvation, for mortal means will not rout death."[8] Salvation can only come from God. It has always belonged to God, and that has not changed.

---

[4] Someone once asked Charles Spurgeon to define a Calvinist. His response was, "The one who says, 'salvation is of the LORD.'"
[5] Keller, 80.
[6] Duguid, 27.
[7] T. Desmond Alexander, *Jonah* Tyndale Old Testament Commentaries, Volume 23a (Downers Grove: IVP, 1988), 117.
[8] Paulinus of Nola, *Poem 26* Ancient Christian Commentary on Scripture, Volume 14 (Downers Grove: IVP, 2003), 139.

According to Ephesians 2, man is dead in his sin.[9] A dead man cannot do the simplest of tasks. He cannot walk. He cannot eat. He cannot play on his phone. He cannot choose between an apple and a cupcake. He is dead, and there is no life in him. So, how is a dead man going to choose God? He cannot. Salvation does not belong to the man. Salvation belongs only to the LORD. Therefore, when the Holy Spirit enters your cold, dead heart, life is breathed into you, giving you the desire to choose God. Praise God that salvation belongs to Him alone, for our cold, dead hearts can do nothing towards our own salvation.

What does it mean when we say that "Salvation is of God and God alone?" If man, dead in his sins, can do anything to achieve salvation, including "choosing" God, then salvation would be of God *and* man. This would mean that man's approval of God's choice and man's acceptance of that choice would be required for his salvation. And if man failed to act, he would thwart God's will. Nothing could be further from the truth. The Holy Spirit is imparted on God's chosen people and enables them to praise God. Additionally, if salvation is of God, and He has saved us, through no actions of our own, we can never lose our salvation.[10]

God used this whole incident to return Jonah to his original call. God not only brought Jonah back to life, but He restored him to the office of prophet. While Jonah had been in the fish praying, the fish had been swimming east. Jonah was now emotionally and spiritually prepared to go to Nineveh to share the gospel with the pagan Ninevites. Surely, going to a city that you hate must be better than being inside a fish.[11] He now, perhaps for the first time, realized that God is sovereign and must be served. His heart, though, was still on the hardened side.

---

[9] Ephesians 2:1-2, "And you were dead in the trespasses and sins in which you once walked, following the course of this world, following the prince of the power of the air, the spirit that is now at work in the sons of disobedience."

[10] John 10:28, "I give them eternal life, and they will never perish, and no one will snatch them out of my hand."

[11] At least you would smell better.

Jonah's theology was mixed up.[12] He was confused about election[13] because he thought that being part of God's chosen people was a matter of ethnicity and outward conformity. Jonah believed that election divided the world into privileged insiders and reprobate outsiders. In Jonah's mind, salvation belonged to the Lord, but the LORD belonged to His people and not to foreigners or sinners.

The Sovereignty of God
Sinclair Ferguson said that "few principles are more important in the Christian life than the practical recognition of the sovereign God, and His gracious determination to draw us near to Himself, whatever the cost may be."[14] By definition, God must be sovereign. He cannot need anyone or anything to rule the universe. No decision can trump God's will. God is God, and we are not. God uses that sovereignty to bring us to Himself. And that is what He did for Jonah.

God was not condemning Jonah by having him swallowed by the fish. He was, however, chastising him for fleeing to Tarshish. God, in His sovereignty, knew exactly what Jonah needed to be ready to preach to Nineveh. And in just a few verses, Jonah came to understand that his sufferings had a purpose. He began to understand that his physical needs were not nearly as important as his relationship with God. His relationship with his God must be his first priority. That relationship should sustain him. And that is something that we all need. We don't need to get bogged down by the stuff of earth; instead, we need to focus on our relationship with our Creator. We must focus on the real (eternal) world, not this temporary physical one.

What did God accomplish in Jonah's Narrowing? Did God have a reason for it, or was it simply punitive? One of the goals of the LORD'S discipline is for His wayward children to repent. The pagan sailors in chapter 1 turned to the LORD. However, Jonah, God's chosen prophet, did not. Jonah fled from the LORD at the beginning of chapter 1, was disciplined at the end of chapter 1, but after three days, still had not repented.

The problem is that Jonah, even after being immersed in fish guts for three days, still harbored sin in his heart. Despite all that God had done to bring Jonah back to Him, deep down, Jonah had not changed. He still hated the

---

[12] Duguid, 28-29.

[13] Election is the doctrine that states that God has already chosen who will be saved and that His grace will bring people to that end.

[14] Ferguson, 39.

Assyrians. Nowhere in the book does it say that Jonah repented. There is no evidence of a changed heart. And, like many of us, he hid the true condition of his heart.

There is a similarity between Jonah and the older brother in the parable of the Prodigal Son in Luke 15:11-32. Henri Nouwen, in his book *Return of the Prodigal Son*, postulates that everyone is each of the characters in the parable at some point in their lives. During our times of rebellion, we are the prodigal son. When we have wayward children, we play the role of the father. And when we look down at others in self-righteousness, we are the older brother. This is the position in which Jonah placed himself. He was self-righteous and believed that only God's chosen people, the Israelites, should receive God's mercy. Have you ever felt like this? Have you ever looked across the pews on a Sunday morning and judged others because of their dress, culture, or sins?

Why do we refuse to show mercy to others when we have received mercy ourselves? The condition of our hearts is absolutely terrible.[15] What can we do about this? How can we become less like Jonah? On our own, there is nothing we can do about the condition of our hearts. We must ask God to make the change. Scripture is full of examples of God changing the hearts of man. Note that God does not fix the sinful heart, but He replaces it with a new heart bent towards Him. Psalm 51:10-12[16] is the prayer of repentance by David when his sin with Bathsheba had been discovered. In it, David asks God to create a clean heart in Him. David is unable to change his sinful heart, but God will not only give him a new, clean heart but also will place His Holy Spirit in David's heart. Ezekiel 36:26-27[17] provides us with greater detail of God's business with our hearts. In this passage, God promises to create a new heart and put the Holy Spirit in those who come to Him in repentance. But

---

[15] Jeremiah 17:9, "The heart is deceitful above all things, and desperately sick; who can understand it?"

[16] Psalm 51:10-12, "Create in me a clean heart, O God, and renew a right spirit within me. [11] Cast me not away from your presence and take not your Holy Spirit from me. [12] Restore to me the joy of your salvation, and uphold me with a willing spirit."

[17] Ezekiel 36:26-27, "And I will give you a new heart, and a new spirit I will put within you. And I will remove the heart of stone from your flesh and give you a heart of flesh. And I will put my Spirit within you and cause you to walk in my statutes and be careful to obey my rules."

then, Ezekiel continues, saying that God will remove the heart of stone and replace it with a heart of flesh. Our cold, dead hearts will be replaced with hearts of flesh, beating only for the One that has forgiven us through His mercy.

The Vomiting

In ancient times, the sea was depicted in a negative way. It symbolized chaos and death. Gentile nations believed that many of their gods lived in the sea. Sea monsters such as Rahab[18] and Leviathan[19] were thought to live just beneath the depths and would take human life whenever they pleased. While these were foreign myths, the Israelites acted as though there was some truth in them. But Jonah's fish story showed that God was in control of what occurred in the sea. In Jonah 1:17,[20] God sent the fish to swallow Jonah. Then after the fish had carried him back to the shores of Canaan,[21] God commanded the fish to vomit him up.[22] The seas were not some sort of unmanageable chaos where God had no power or influence, as taught by pagan belief systems. The seas, like the rest of creation, fall under the sovereignty of God. The story of Jonah emphasizes God's sovereignty.

Verse 10 tells us that the fish vomited Jonah out upon dry land. If you have ever had a child who was sick to their stomach, you know that vomiting is disgusting. But it serves a purpose to remove harmful substances or poisons from our bodies. In Leviticus 18:28,[23] the LORD told the Israelites that the Promised Land would vomit them out if they continued in their sins. The word "vomit" is appropriate in Leviticus 18 because God was disgusted with Israel's sins. The use of the term in Jonah implies that Jonah, in his sinful state, was disgusting to both God and the fish. As a result, the fish vomited him out. This was likely on the coast of Canaan, somewhere near Joppa, some 500 miles from Nineveh.

---

[18] Isaiah 51:9b-10, "Was it not you who cut Rahab in pieces, who pierced the dragon? Was it not you who dried up the sea, the waters of the great deep, who made the depths of the sea a way for the redeemed to pass over?"

[19] Psalm 74:14, "You crushed the heads of Leviathan; you gave him as food for the creatures of the wilderness."

[20] Jonah 1:17, "And the LORD appointed a great fish to swallow up Jonah. And Jonah was in the belly of the fish three days and three nights."

[21] The fish likely dropped Jonah near Joppa, some 500 miles from Nineveh.

[22] In Jonah 2:10, God spoke and the fish listened, understood, and obeyed. Unlike Jonah, who listened, understood, and disobeyed.

[23] Leviticus 18:28, "Lest the land vomit you out when you make it unclean, as it vomited out the nation that was before you."

We can learn from Jonah's experience in the fish. We need to have God's Word written upon our hearts so that when we are in distress, we can turn with confidence to the words of God for comfort. God may place us in our own Narrowing to make us realize our need for Him and turn to Him in repentance. The end result of a Narrowing is a renewal of our faith in God. When we go through times of suffering and discomfort, we need to trust that God has a purpose in placing us there.

Salvation belongs to the LORD. As such, it rescues runaway prophets, violent foreign capitals, prodigal sons and their older brothers, those who have committed moral failures, and those who seem unworthy to be saved. No part of salvation depends on man, or none of us would be saved. Therefore, praise God that our eternal destiny lies in God's sovereign will and not in our own vain attempts to save ourselves.

Chapter 6 Discussion Questions

1. What did it mean, in Jonah 2:7, that Jonah's prayers came to the LORD in His holy temple? What is God's holy temple? Does it exist today?

2. How did the LORD'S holy temple provide Jonah with hope?

3. What had Jonah vowed to God that he needed to repay?

4. How does Jonah 2:10 display God's sovereignty?

5. What does the phrase "Salvation belongs to the LORD" mean?

6. Why do you think that Jonah waited until he was at his lowest point before he prayed? Have you ever been guilty of this?

7. What is the best way to hear from God? Do you make a practice of it?

8. Did Jonah's time in the fish prepare him to witness to Nineveh? If so, how?

7

The Call

JONAH 3:1-4

Then the word of the LORD came to Jonah the second time, saying, ² "Arise, go to Nineveh, that great city, and call out against it the message that I tell you." ³ So Jonah arose and went to Nineveh, according to the word of the LORD. Now Nineveh was an exceedingly great city, three days' journey in breadth. ⁴ Jonah began to go into the city, going a day's journey. And he called out, "Yet forty days, and Nineveh shall be overthrown!"

MANY OF US REMEMBER THE events of September 11, 2001, quite well. We were shocked when the planes slammed into the twin towers of the World Trade Center. We watched in horror the events at the Pentagon. We applauded the actions of the heroes on flight 93 who wrestled control from the hijackers and crashed in a field in Somerset County, PA, but potentially saved the lives of thousands of civilians. If you were alive, you likely remember where you were when you heard the news. One of the great things that came out of the September 11 tragedy was the unity of our country. For the first time in decades, people of different cultures, belief systems, political sides, and religions all came together to help our neighbors and heal. Millions committed to pray for healing for our country. This is not anything new, as tragedies often result in some sort of revival. Before Jonah visited Nineveh, the city experienced a series of famines, plagues, revolts, and a solar eclipse.[1] Each of these things was considered an omen of worse things to come. The Ninevites were ripe and ready for the spiritual harvest of revival. The LORD had been preparing the hearts of the Ninevites to repent and turn to Him. Jonah's call to Nineveh was the catalyst for this miraculous revival.

Jonah's Restoration

Jonah 3:1-2 tells us that "the word of the LORD came to Jonah…" And this time, when the word of the LORD came to Jonah, he arose and went. Jonah had been reinstated as a prophet by the grace of God. Says Duguid, "The LORD has an uncomfortable habit of continuing to use seriously flawed presentations to bring people to faith in Christ."[2] Jonah will resume his office in obedience and with a sense of duty. He will implicitly obey his God. However, there was still no evidence of repentance in Jonah's heart.

This brings up an important question: How does God respond when men of God sin? Jonah was a prophet of God. As such, he mediated between God and His people. To mediate successfully, Jonah had to be on good terms with both sides. Therefore, he had to fully obey God's every command. As we have seen, he did not.[3] Jonah's eight-word (five in Hebrew) message to the Ninevites was an example of minimalism. Joah did the minimum that God asked of him and no more. He still hated the Ninevites and didn't care if they were saved.

---

[1] John H. Walton, *Jonah* TEBC. (Grand Rapids: Zondervan, 2008), 483.
[2] Duguid, 42.
[3] Jonah was not on the best of terms with either God or Nineveh.

For a man of God to be restored to ministry, he must repent of his sins,[4] be forgiven,[5] and show that he can once again be trusted.[6] The first two steps, repentance and forgiveness, can be accomplished in a relatively short time. Forgiveness is instantaneous. However, it can take years to fully earn someone's trust back. To be restored to ministry can be even more difficult, if not impossible.

In the Book of Jonah, Jonah never repented and we have no evidence that God ever forgave him. Yet God restored Jonah to office. God was able to forgive Jonah without Jonah's repentance. What then, of Jonah earning back God's trust? Did Jonah need to have God's trust? Was it necessary for the task to which God called him? God did not need to be able to trust Jonah. In fact, God did not need Jonah at all. God could have brought Nineveh to repentance without Jonah or any other prophet. God does not *need* man to save anyone. Salvation belongs to the LORD. However, God typically brings men to saving faith through other men. God didn't need to trust Jonah, Jonah needed to trust God. God wanted Jonah to go to Nineveh because He was working on Jonah's cold heart.[7]

Jonah hadn't repented, been forgiven, or re-established trust, but God still used him to bring the salvation of the Ninevites. If God can use Jonah in this position, He can use us without theologically sound doctrine and slick presentation skills. All that is needed for effective evangelism to occur is the presence of the Holy Spirit. "If God has chosen and called you, He will not

---

[4] Acts 3:19, "Repent therefore, and turn back, that your sins may be blotted out." Jeremiah 15:19a, "Therefore thus says the LORD: If you return, I will restore you, and you shall stand before me." Proverbs 28:13, "Whoever conceals his transgressions will not prosper, but he who confesses and forsakes them will obtain mercy."

[5] Luke 6:37, "Judge not, and you will not be judged; condemn not, and you will not be condemned; forgive, and you will be forgiven." Matthew 5:23-24, "So if you are offering your gift at the altar and there remember that your brother has something against you, leave your gift there before the altar and go. First be reconciled to your brother and then come and offer your gift." Matthew 6:14-15, "For if you forgive others their trespasses, your heavenly Father will also forgive you, but if you do not forgive others their trespasses, neither will your Father forgive your trespasses." Psalm 103:10-12, "He does not deal with us according to our sins, nor repay us according to our iniquities. For as high as the heavens are above the earth, so great is His steadfast love toward those who fear Him; as far as the east is from the west, so far does He remove our transgressions from us."

[6] John 11:8, "She said, "No one, LORD." And Jesus said, "Neither do I condemn you; go, and from now on sin no more." Proverbs 11:3, "The integrity of the upright guides them, but the crookedness of the treacherous destroys them." Psalm 15:1-2, "O LORD, who shall sojourn in your tent? Who shall dwell on your holy hill? He who walks blamelessly and does what is right and speaks truth in his heart."

[7] There are other reasons for sending Jonah to Nineveh, not the least of which is the salvation of 120,000 souls.

give you up; He is at work in you and will complete that great work on the last day."[8]

Jonah 3:1-2[9] contains God's second call to Jonah. It is almost word for word as his first call in Jonah 1:1-2.[10] As parents, we often have to repeat directions to our children. With one of our kids, we learned that there could be "too many words." We would tell him to "Please take your shoes to your room," over and over, but this eventually was shortened to "Shoes! Room! Shoes! Room!" It can be difficult to repeatedly ask them to do something while remaining loving and patient. But God continued to call Jonah to Nineveh with infinite patience. God, in His grace, has given Jonah a second chance. So, it is for all who repent and cry out to the LORD. Many Christians say that it took a second or third exposure to the gospel before they began a relationship with God. Finally, Jonah is willing and able to bring God's message to Nineveh. But his heart remained unchanged.

Why Nineveh? Why Jonah?
In Jonah 1 and 3, God called Nineveh a great city. This shows that Nineveh was extremely important to God and indicates why God wanted to spare it. Jonah was at odds with God's desire to spare Nineveh. He had never wanted to preach there. Knowing Nineveh would be destroyed if he didn't go, Jonah was guilty of their murder in his heart. But like all sinners, Jonah justified his callous attitude with three excuses. First, Nineveh was a known enemy of Israel.[11] Secondly, Nineveh was extremely violent, and Jonah's safety was not guaranteed. Lastly, the size of Nineveh was around 120,000 people. There would be no way he could ever reach that many people. However, in all of this, Jonah was not alone. This was not something that Jonah could handle on his own. Jonah's mission would be challenging. It would require supernatural intervention to succeed.[12] He had the One who would be his shield and

---

[8] Duguid, 44.
[9] Jonah 3:1-2, "Then the word of the LORD came to Jonah the second time, saying, 'Arise, go to Nineveh, that great city, and call out against it the message that I tell you.'"
[10] Jonah 1:1-2, "Now the word of the LORD came to Jonah the son of Amittai, saying, 'Arise, go to Nineveh, that great city, and call out against it, for their evil has come up before me.'"
[11] Philip Cary, *Jonah* Brazos Commentary (Grand Rapids: Brazos, 2008), 40.
[12] Jonah's mission is similar to yours and mine. We are called to make disciples of all nations. We, too, will need supernatural intervention if we are to succeed.

strength accompanying him. Nothing but complete reliance on God would get him through this assignment. It is the same way with us. We are warned repeatedly throughout Scripture against trying to succeed on our own strength. Incapable of saving even ourselves, how can we expect to save others outside of God's power and grace?

From a human perspective, Jonah certainly was not the ideal person to preach to Nineveh, not in the least because he'd just come from the insides of a fish![13] After reading Jonah 4, it is clear that Jonah's heart was not where it should have been. Jonah still hated the Ninevites. 1 Samuel 16:7[14] tells us that God looks at a person's heart. God knew the exact condition of Jonah's heart. But also, God knew how the Ninevites would respond to Jonah's message of destruction. God knew Jonah's message would be enough to spur Nineveh on to repentance. And so, God sent Jonah, His holy runaway, calloused and murderous heart and all, to preach the "good news"[15] to the great city of Nineveh.

So far in our story, Jonah practiced the opposite of "loving one's enemies." He had no compassion for the Ninevites. Jonah would have rather died than pray for the Ninevites. Jonah was not fond of the Assyrians. In fact, he hated them, and they probably weren't too fond of him either. Having been deeply impacted by his adventures on the seas, Jonah is now going to obey God, but he was not pleased about it. However, salvation is not just for those on our side.

Jonah's Message
In verse 2,[16] God instructed Jonah to deliver "the message that I tell you." God's command made it clear that the message was not Jonah's. In John 12:49, Jesus says, "For I have not spoken on my own authority, but the Father who sent me has Himself given me a commandment—what to say and what to speak." It was the same with Jonah. He did not speak on his own authority. In Jonah 2:9, Jonah declared that "Salvation belongs to the LORD." Salvation is all God's doing. Jonah did not get to decide who would be saved and who

---

[13] I hope he bathed before he preached to Nineveh.
[14] 1 Samuel 16:7, "But the LORD said to Samuel, "Do not look on his appearance or on the height of his stature, because I have rejected him. For the LORD sees not as man sees. Man looks on the outward appearance, but *the LORD looks on the heart*." (italics added)
[15] OK, perhaps it wasn't good news. It was a message of doom. But the end result was good. So the news brought about good.
[16] Jonah 3:2, "Arise, go to Nineveh, that great city, and call out against it the message that I tell you."

would not. It wasn't his call. It was God's. And God had predestined the Ninevites to repent and be forgiven.

The Holy Spirit went ahead of Jonah and prepared the hearts of the Ninevites. He also gave Jonah's message the power necessary to impact this evil and violent city. Jonah's message came from God, and the Ninevites recognized this. God used Jonah's imperfect message, biases, flaws, and all, to save the great city of Nineveh. The message is one of the central themes of Jonah: God bringing life from death. "It was out of Jonah's inner death that life was born in Nineveh."[17] However, Jonah was still not humble in his call to Nineveh. He still displayed that same sense of self-righteousness when ministering to Nineveh as shown by his angry outburst in Jonah 4.

Verse 4 provides us with his message, "Yet forty days, and Nineveh shall be overthrown!" His entire message was five words in Hebrew. It was kind of underwhelming. Jonah did the bare minimum when he obeyed God. However, the word "overthrown" is based on the Hebrew word *neh-pā-ket*, which is the same word used in Genesis 19,[18] where God destroyed Sodom and Gomorrah. This indicates that Nineveh was not going to be overthrown by an enemy but destroyed by God. Based on that definition, the Ninevites would have clearly understood the complete destruction in store for them.

Jonah's message was not focused on anything other than the destruction of Nineveh. There was no talk of mercy, grace, repentance, or salvation.[19] Jonah's message could have been *"Unless Nineveh repents*, it will be overthrown in forty days." God's pronouncement of judgment against Nineveh's sin did not hold out the possibility that judgment might be delayed, mitigated, or avoided.[20] While God's mercy was missing from Jonah's message, it can be inferred, based on God's character, that God could show

---

[17] Ferguson, 55.
[18] Genesis 19:21, "He said to him, "Behold, I grant you this favor also, that I will not *overthrow* the city of which you have spoken." Genesis 19:25, "And he *overthrew* those cities, and all the valley, and all the inhabitants of the cities, and what grew on the ground." Genesis 19:29, "So it was that, when God destroyed the cities of the valley, God remembered Abraham and sent Lot out of the midst of the *overthrow* when He *overthrew* the cities in which Lot had lived." (italics added)
[19] John Calvin postulated that Jonah left the aspects of grace, repentance, and salvation out of the message on purpose. (Calvin, *Commentaries,* 134).
[20] Timmer, 98.

them mercy. Jonah clearly understood this because in Jonah 4:2[21] he complained that he knew God would relent from the planned destruction. Therefore, Jonah's omission of this call to repentance and offer of God's mercy is significant. This goes beyond delivering the minimalist sermon that he preached. This shows that Jonah still had no compassion for the Ninevites and didn't care if they were destroyed.

We are very much like Jonah; we are very good at proclaiming judgment on those we dislike. We are also excellent at withholding grace from those who need it most. We need to approach the throne of God and ask Him to create in us new hearts. Our hearts of stone desperately need to be replaced with hearts of flesh, full of His love and compassion for the lost, regardless of who they are.

God's Judgment
God, in His mercy, allowed the Ninevites time for repentance. This is what God does. This is who God is. Think about it: when we sin, we deserve death. But God allows us to continue living so that there will be time for us to repent. 2 Peter 3:9 tells us that "the LORD is not slow to fulfill His promise as some count slowness, but is patient toward you, not wishing that any should perish, but that all should reach repentance." God's grace and mercy were something that the Ninevites had never experienced: God's willingness to await repentance while delaying judgment. This was vastly different from the false gods of the time. Those gods demanded obedience and sacrifice. There was never any display of mercy with their people. How could there be? They were objects of stone, metal, and imagination.

Because of the work of the Holy Spirit, the Ninevites enthusiastically repented despite Jonah's half-hearted message. The Ninevites responded even before Jonah could finish his brief sermon. Jonah had hardly started before the Ninevites began to repent. They repeated the message around the city until even the king heard it. Daniel Timmer says, "Far from removing any motivation to serve God, as long as one comes to see one's own sinfulness, the account of Nineveh's repentance and God's merciful response to it is a wonderful encouragement to throw oneself on God's mercy, which is offered

---

[21] Jonah 4:2, "And he prayed to the LORD and said, "O LORD, is not this what I said when I was yet in my country? That is why I made haste to flee to Tarshish; for I knew that you are a gracious God and merciful, slow to anger and abounding in steadfast love, and relenting from disaster."

in full accord with His justice on the basis of Christ's cross-work."[22] "Although Nineveh was not overturned, it did experience a turn-around."[23]

This was the second time in Jonah that Gentiles repented and Jonah had not. What about those, like Jonah, who refuse to repent? How shall we respond to them? According to Caesarius of Arles, "we should not despair of those who are still unwilling to correct their vices and do not even blush to defend them."[24] Let us turn from our sin and repent. Whether they repent or not, let us be sure to do so.[25]

So, what about when pastors fall today? It seems increasingly frequent today that pastors are being disqualified from ministry. We should not be surprised by this, as those who undertake servanthood to God can expect to be prime targets of the enemy. Jonah 3 provides us with insight on God's response to sin in the life of His servants. God, in His Word, tells us what is expected of church leaders. 1 Timothy 3:1-7[26] and Titus 1:5-9[27] provide the qualifications for ministers, and the bar is set pretty high. The reason for this is that those who are called to lead God's people must set a standard for

---

[22] Timmer, 114-115.
[23] Edwin M. Good, *Irony in the Old Testament* (Philadelphia: Westminster, 1965), 48.
[24] Caesarius of Arles, *Sermon 133.3* Ancient Christian Commentary on Scripture, Volume 14 (Downers Grove: IVP, 2003), 140.
[25] Philippians 2:12, "Therefore, my beloved, as you have always obeyed, so now, not only as in my presence but much more in my absence, work out your own salvation with fear and trembling."
[26] 1 Timothy 3:1-7, "The saying is trustworthy: If anyone aspires to the office of overseer, he desires a noble task. Therefore, an overseer must be above reproach, the husband of one wife, sober-minded, self-controlled, respectable, hospitable, able to teach, not a drunkard, not violent but gentle, not quarrelsome, not a lover of money. He must manage his own household well, with all dignity keeping his children submissive, for if someone does not know how to manage his own household, how will he care for God's church? He must not be a recent convert, or he may become puffed up with conceit and fall into the condemnation of the devil. Moreover, he must be well thought of by outsiders, so that he may not fall into disgrace, into a snare of the devil."
[27] Titus 1:5-9, "This is why I left you in Crete, so that you might put what remained into order, and appoint elders in every town as I directed you— if anyone is above reproach, the husband of one wife, and his children are believers and not open to the charge of debauchery or insubordination. For an overseer, as God's steward, must be above reproach. He must not\ be arrogant or quick-tempered or a drunkard or violent or greedy for gain, but hospitable, a lover of good, self-controlled, upright, holy, and disciplined. He must hold firm to the trustworthy word as taught, so that he may be able to give instruction in sound doctrine and also to rebuke those who contradict it."

morality and ethics that is above reproach as to not hinder God's message with their behavior.

How does God respond when a pastor is sexually unfaithful or financially irresponsible? God responds to pastors who sin just as He does to all who sin. If they repent, they will be forgiven.[28] However, there is more to it than that. Sin has consequences, and even if the pastor has repented and been forgiven, he will still have to face those consequences. This might include public confession of sin, church discipline, or stepping down from the pulpit. That doesn't mean that the pastor can never return to ministry. He must seek forgiveness and establish trust with those he has wronged. How should we respond when pastors fall? Five fundamental truths must be understood.

1. Pastors will come under spiritual attack. John 15:20-22[29] tells us that we will be hated by the world. Pastors even more so. They are "high value targets" in the sight of the enemy.
2. As such, pastors will sin publicly. Pastors are human, and all humans sin. None of us are exempt, even pastors.
3. Pastors are not God. They are His representatives, but they are not Him. Just because a pastor sins publicly does not mean Christianity is untrue. If anything, it is more valid because it shows us that sin has affected every area of this fallen world, and only the blood of Jesus Christ is enough to save it.
4. We all sin and all sin can be forgiven. Just as our sins need to be forgiven, so do those of our pastors. We are to forgive them when they repent.[30]
5. Pastors can be restored to office. Trust must be re-established, and that will take time. During that time, we are to love and support them. Continued oversight may be required to ensure that he does not fall into sin again. One of the most important things for fallen pastors is the love of family and friends. Let's be sure they get it by responding in love to our brothers in Christ.

---

[28] 1 John 1:9, "If we confess our sins, He is faithful and just to forgive us our sins and to cleanse us from all unrighteousness."

[29] John 15:20-22, "Remember the word that I said to you: 'A servant is not greater than his master.' If they persecuted me, they will also persecute you. If they kept my word, they will also keep yours. But all these things they will do to you on account of my name, because they do not know Him who sent me. If I had not come and spoken to them, they would not have been guilty of sin, but now they have no excuse for their sin."

[30] While we are called to forgive our brothers and sisters in Christ when they repent, sometimes distance is needed for those impacted by their sin.

Let us show ourselves to be like the people of Nineveh. We, like the Ninevites, are sinners who cannot save ourselves apart from the blood of Jesus Christ. We live in a culture that rejects God and religion and yet relentlessly pursues the false idols of wealth, power, social status, and pleasure. We must repent and turn to God in faith. Only by doing so can we experience eternal life with our Savior. Unlike the Ninevites, who were given 40 days to repent, we are not guaranteed years, months, or even days. We must repent now. Tomorrow is not promised.

Chapter 7 Discussion Questions

1. How does the story of Jonah show us that we cannot save ourselves?

2. Why did God restore Jonah to the office of prophet when he never repented?

3. Do you think Jonah preached all that God told him to? Why or why not? Does it matter?

4. How did Jonah's message display the hardness of his heart?

5. How are we to respond when men of God fall?

6. What steps are necessary for a pastor to be restored to ministry?

7. Nineveh had 40 days to repent. The number 40 in Hebrew is often associated with periods of religious significance. What are some other uses of the number 40 in Scripture?

8

Repenting

JONAH 3:5-9

And the people of Nineveh believed God. They called for a fast an put on sackcloth, from the greatest of them to the least of them. ⁶ The word reached the king of Nineveh, and he arose from his throne, removed his robe, covered himself with sackcloth, and sat in ashes. ⁷ And he issued a proclamation and published through Nineveh, "By the decree of the king and his nobles: Let neither man nor beast, herd nor flock, taste anything. Let them not feed or drink water, ⁸ but let man and beast be covered with sackcloth and let them call out mightily to God. Let everyone turn from his evil way and from the violence that is in his hands. ⁹ Who knows? God may turn and relent and turn from His fierce anger, so that we may not perish."

SOME TIME AGO, IT WAS discovered that a pastor friend was addicted to pornography, which led to him using an app designed to facilitate people cheating on their spouses. When confronted by church leadership, he was motivated to change because he feared losing his marriage, job, and reputation in the community. He was sorry that he had been caught in sin, but he didn't hate the sin itself. After some time, his sexual sins returned and he was back to his previous ways. Eventually, his wife filed for divorce and his pastoral ministry ended. What is the difference between my friend and King David when he was confronted with his sins of adultery and murder by the prophet Nathan?[1] The difference is that my friend merely regretted his sin. He never truly repented. David repented of his sin, turned from his sins and turned back to God. As a result, God forgave David. God's forgiveness requires true repentance.

In Jonah 3:5-9, the people of Nineveh believed God and repented. What does it mean to repent? A simple definition of repentance is a change of behavior from worse to better. But there is a whole lot more to it than that. As we have previously discussed, repentance is a two-step process. It involves turning away from one's sins and then turning toward God in faith. The Westminster Confession of Faith 15.2 says, "In this repentance, the sinner is able to see his sins as God sees them, as filthy and hateful, and as involving great danger to the sinner, because they are completely contrary to the holy nature and righteous law of God. Understanding that God in Christ is merciful to those who repent, the sinner suffers deep sorrow for and hates his sins, and so he determines to turn away from all of them. And turning to God, he tries to walk with Him according to all His commandments."

The Hebrew word for repent is *shub*, which means to turn. According to Sinclair Ferguson, "It is about turning back to God. It is about returning to His grace."[2] *Shub* is used in chapter 3 of Jonah twice, once in verse 8[3] and

---

[1] 2 Samuel 12:7-9, "Nathan said to David, "You are the man! Thus says the LORD, the God of Israel, 'I anointed you king over Israel, and I delivered you out of the hand of Saul. And I gave you your master's house and your master's wives into your arms and gave you the house of Israel and of Judah. And if this were too little, I would add to you as much more. Why have you despised the word of the LORD, to do what is evil in His sight? You have struck down Uriah the Hittite with the sword and have taken his wife to be your wife and have killed him with the sword of the Ammonites."

[2] Sinclair Ferguson, *Faithful God: An Exposition of the Book of Ruth* (Darlington: Evangelical Press, 2013), 21.

[3] Jonah 3:8, "But let man and beast be covered with sackcloth and let them call out mightily to God. Let everyone *turn* from his evil way and from the violence that is in his hands." (italics added)

once in verse 9.[4] In verse 8, it is the Ninevites who *turn* from their sin. In verse 9, God *turns* from His anger against the Ninevites. The turning of man led to the turning of God. However, God is the one who has to begin the process of turning man. If man is dead in his sins, he cannot turn from his sins on his own strength. He needs the Holy Spirit in his heart to do so. Says Calvin, "Repentance consists not in these eternal things: for God cares not for outward rites, and all those things which are resplendent in the sight of men are worthless before Him; what indeed, He requires, is sincerity of heart."[5] Sincere hearts repent. Repentance is always an act of God. The apostle Paul tells us in 2 Timothy 2:25b-26, "God may perhaps grant them repentance leading to a knowledge of the truth, and they may come to their senses and escape from the snare of the devil, after being captured by Him to do His will."

Repentance is not the same as regret. Regret is feeling sorry for being caught in sin. Repentance is being sorry that you sinned then turning to God for forgiveness. Regret is more concerned about the consequences and punishment than the sin that brought them about. This is worldly sorrow as opposed to godly sorrow. Worldly sorrow says, "I'm sorry I got caught." This is self-consumed sorrow. Godly sorrow says, "I'm sorry I have sinned." Godly sorrow aches at the loss of communion with God and fervently seeks to be restored to His favor. The key to true repentance is a change of heart and soul. It is the "making of a new heart and of a right spirit."[6] Repentance says, "Create in me a clean heart, O God, and renew a right spirit within me."[7] Fittingly, David's prayer of repentance after sinning with Bathsheba and having Uriah murdered is an excellent example of Godly sorrow over our sin. Repentance is so much more than regretting sin. It is experiencing God's forgiveness and restoration of sweet communion with Him. However, it is also a turning away from sin. Repentance grounded in regret, but without a change of heart, will not last. Those faithful to God will live a life of repentance. David's close communion with God led him to understand the

---

[4] Jonah 3:9, "Who knows? God may turn and relent and *turn* from His fierce anger, so that we may not perish." (italics added)
[5] Calvin, *Commentaries,* 103-104.
[6] Martin, 271.
[7] Psalm 51:10-13, "Create in me a clean heart, O God, and renew a right spirit within me. [11] Cast me not away from your presence and take not your Holy Spirit from me. Restore to me the joy of your salvation and uphold me with a willing spirit. Then I will teach transgressors your ways, and sinners will return to you."

sacrifice God requires for forgiveness: a broken and contrite heart and spirit.[8] And contrite hearts are what the Ninevites displayed with their immediate actions of a people in mourning.

What about Jonah? The text doesn't say that he regretted his sin, much less repented. But in Jonah 3 we have an unrepentant prophet who brought countless others to repentance. God could have saved Nineveh without Jonah, but He didn't. Even though Jonah didn't repent, God used him to affect the salvation of Nineveh anyway.

Nineveh's Repentance
The people of Nineveh took God at His word, turned from their evil ways, and repented. They understood that they were deservedly facing judgment on account of their wicked, violent lives. Even though Jonah's message never mentioned repentance, Nineveh was convicted by what they heard and repented accordingly. There was no hesitation on behalf of the Ninevites. Their response was immediate and city-wide. According to Chrysostom, "the fornicator became chaste; the bold man meek; the grasping and extortionate moderate and kind; and the slothful industrious."[9] There was a noticeable difference in the lives of the Ninevites before and after Jonah's message. They received new hearts, alive in God. They became who they were created to be.

In verse 5, it says that the Ninevites believed God. The Hebrew word for "believe," *way·ya 'ă·mî·nū,* expresses the idea of a deep, personal trust in someone. The Ninevites displayed the sincerity of their conversion in the steps they took to repent: a strict fast and sackcloth and ashes for all, including livestock. Jonah 3 does not say if the conversion of Nineveh was only a passing thing. We don't know if there was any lasting fruit from their conversion. But we know their repentance was real and their response caused God to relent from destroying their city.[10]

Nineveh repented for several different reasons. The first was the person of Jonah. Jonah came from Israel, a sworn enemy of Nineveh. He would have

---

[8] Psalm 51:17, "The sacrifices of God are a broken spirit; a broken and contrite heart, O God, you will not despise."
[9] Chrysostom, 145.
[10] In less than 100 years, the Assyrian (Ninevite) army would destroy the ten northern tribes of Israel. (722 B.C.)

no reason outside of God's call to preach to them. The only reason that Jonah was there was because God commanded him to go. Jonah stood to gain nothing other than God's favor. He did not want the Ninevites to repent. He wanted them to face the wrath of God. Jonah was hoping for judgment, not grace, and his message reflected this.[11]

Another reason for Ninevite repentance was that when Jonah came, Nineveh was in turmoil under the Assyrian kings Ashur-dan III and Ashur-nirari V. Since the Assyrian throne had grown weak, the rule of the country had fallen to five different governors. While Nineveh was experiencing military vulnerability, there were earthquakes, famine, revolts, plagues, and solar eclipses.[12] The climate of fear and unrest was a major element in the Ninevites' repentance.[13] Any of these things would have predisposed Nineveh to repent. However, the combination of several would have prepared their hearts to heed Jonah's call. These events would have made Jonah's message far more believable than if he had preached it without those events ever occurring. "The state of affairs would have made both rulers and subjects unusually attuned to the message of a visiting prophet."[14]

The actions of the Ninevite king were another reason for the city's repentance. The king served God by compelling all of Nineveh to repent. Like the fish following God's sovereign will, the Ninevite king did the same. He demanded that all of Nineveh "turn from his evil way and from the violence in their hands."[15] Turning from evil would have been a foreign concept to the Ninevites. However, when the king commanded that the city repent, and he himself began repenting, the people grew frightened and willingly followed his example.[16] To do so, the king had to be willing to admit that he, too, was

---

[11] Jonah 3:4, "Yet forty days, and Nineveh shall be overthrown!"
[12] Assyrian omen texts warned against events such as solar eclipses, famines, and earthquakes. Solar eclipses indicated that the wrath of the gods was about to be unleashed upon them. Famine and drought indicated a general displeasure with the gods. Earthquakes were seen as a divine omen of a weak military. Combining of any of these events with another indicated that an unparalleled disaster was about to strike the city.
[13] Martin, 264.
[14] Timmer, 94.
[15] Jonah 3:8b, "Let everyone turn from his evil way and from the violence that is in his hands."
[16] There are other instances in Scripture of kings commanding their people to fast. 2 Chronicles 20:3, "Then Jehoshaphat was afraid and set his face to seek the Lord and proclaimed a fast throughout all Judah." Joel 2:15-17, "Blow the trumpet in Zion; consecrate a fast; call a solemn assembly; gather the people. Consecrate the congregation; assemble the elders; gather the children, even nursing infants. Let the bridegroom leave his room, and the bride her chamber. Between the vestibule and the altar let the priests, the ministers of the LORD, weep and say, "Spare your people, O LORD, and make not your heritage a reproach, a byword among the nations. Why should they say among the peoples, 'Where is their God?'"

a sinner. It would be very humiliating for any king to admit that he was sinful and needed to repent to a power higher than his own. Typically, Assyrian kings were full of themselves, bragging about their military victories or building programs. But not this king. He showed human frailty and worthlessness by putting on sackcloth and ashes.[17] He did so to save his people and city.

While those are all good explanations for Nineveh's repentance, ultimately, it occurred because of God's sovereignty working through Jonah's message. The king's decree[18] confirmed what Jonah knew to be true. God can forgive anyone, including this evil city. God is intimately involved in all evangelism. Election guarantees that some of those we evangelize will repent and turn to God. It is not our words that change people's hearts, but the Holy Spirit working in their hearts. The same was true for Jonah, except that the entire city of Nineveh, from the greatest to the least, repented and turned to God. God had chosen to save the city of Nineveh at that particular time.

Fasting and Sackcloth

Jonah 3:7-8[19] includes the king's command about fasting and sackcloth. The king called for the entire city and their animals to put on sackcloth and call out mightily to God. The people of Nineveh obeyed their king and fasted and prayed. Fasting is a powerful tool in the Christian faith. According to the Westminster Confession of Faith 21.5, fasting is to be done "upon special occasions, which are, in their several times and seasons, to be used in a holy and religious manner." Fasting is not to be done as a display of personal piety. Fasting is to be done to focus oneself on God and His promises to us. This is precisely what the citizens of Nineveh did. They fasted and prayed in a holy and religious manner.

---

[17] Alexander, 122.

[18] Jonah 3:9, "Who knows? God may turn and relent and turn from His fierce anger, so that we may not perish,"

[19] Jonah 3:7-8, "And he issued a proclamation and published through Nineveh, 'By the decree of the king and his nobles: Let neither man nor beast, herd nor flock, taste anything. Let them not feed or drink water but let man and beast be covered with sackcloth and let them call out mightily to God. Let everyone turn from his evil way and from the violence that is in his hands.'"

What about the animals? Why did the Ninevite king declare a fast for them as well? The Ninevites did not know that repentance was even an option. The Ninevites were not brought up with the Jewish Scriptures, in which only man was created in God's image.[20] In the Ninevite culture, which was laden with superstition, there was a belief that animals had souls that were directly tied to their human owners.[21] The Ninevites hoped that by having the horses and donkeys fast and wear sackcloth, that God might show them additional mercy and relent from His coming judgment upon them. Says Iain Duguid, "Even though the image of domestic animals in sackcloth outfits is undoubtedly comic, the effect certainly conveys the deadly seriousness of the Ninevites."[22]

Many of us are not likely familiar with sackcloth. Sackcloth is a very coarse, rough fabric woven from animal hair, often worn in times of mourning or penitence. Most likely, sackcloth resembled the hairy mantle used by the Bedouins. Sackcloth was also a way of asking for mercy[23] and was occasionally worn by the prophets.[24] In fact, many of the ancient prophets wore rough garments made of the skins of beasts. Sackcloth is hot, itchy, and horribly uncomfortable to wear. To wear sackcloth symbolized the turning away from worldly comfort. It was a form of self-denial.

Ashes are often used to represent desolation and ruin. The Ninevites' donning of sackcloth and ashes was not a meaningless show. God saw the genuine and humble change of heart represented by the sackcloth and ashes, and in His mercy "relented" and did not bring about His plan to destroy them. It was not the outward actions of fasting, praying, and wearing of sackcloth that caused God to relent. He mercifully relented because the people's hearts had turned from their wicked ways and believed in Him. The wearing of sackcloth and ashes was external evidence of an internal transformation.

---

[20] Genesis 1:27, "So God created man in His own image, in the image of God He created him; male and female He created them."
[21] https://biblehub.com/commentaries/jonah/3-7.htm Accessed October 7, 2024.
[22] Duguid, 42.
[23] In 1 Kings 20:30-32, we have the story of the army of Israel defeating the Assyrian army and the captured Assyrian army asking for mercy, Ben-hadad (the king of Assyria) "fled and entered an inner chamber in the city. And his servants said to him, "Behold now, we have heard that the kings of the house of Israel are merciful kings. Let us put sackcloth around our waists and ropes on our heads and go out to the king of Israel. Perhaps he will spare your life." So they tied sackcloth around their waists and put ropes on their heads and went to the king of Israel and said, "Your servant Ben-hadad says, 'Please, let me live.'" And he said, 'Does he still live? He is my brother.'"
[24] Elijah wore clothing made of animal hair and a leather belt. Scripture does not tell us what type of animal hair it was. John the Baptist wore clothing made of camel's hair.

Before Jonah's proclamation of destruction, Nineveh was dead in its sin. This great city, as mighty and powerful and massive as it was, was dead. And yet, when Jonah came to them and the Holy Spirit was given to them, Nineveh came to life. God also brought Jonah, when he was dead in the belly of the fish, back to life. This is what God does. He brings the dead to life. All living things will ultimately die. And yet, God accomplishes the opposite of what happens in this fallen world, bringing life from worthless ashes.

We would do well to emulate Nineveh. Despite all its advances, our modern world is just as sinful as Nineveh was. Perhaps we don't behead people or cut off their lips, but we have our own sins that are just as repulsive, if not worse. Abortion slaughters millions of babies every year, human trafficking prays upon the most vulnerable, rampant pornography continues to degrade women and hurt our society, and yet we go on with our lives as if those things weren't happening before our very eyes. Nineveh had never heard of the LORD, but we have, and we disobey just as much. Nineveh was ignorant in their sin and yet heeded a foreign God's call and repented. We know of Him and even print our money with a message of reliance upon Him yet continue in our disobedience and sin as if it doesn't matter. Our consciences are seared by constant exposure to sin and our hearts of stone feel no empathy for those most needing His mercy.

We too, must repent of our sins against God and our fellow man. Calvin says, "God daily urges us to repentance, and that is, because He desires to be reconciled to us, and that we should be reconciled to Him."[25] We must fast and pray and ask God to open our eyes to the sin and suffering around us. We must ask God to break our hearts of stone so that we crave His forgiveness more than the empty pleasures of sin. God is not slow in punishing sin. He waits patiently so people will repent. We must do everything we can to warn others with the message, "All have sinned and rebelled against God. Repent and believe!" We cannot afford to remain callous and impenitent. Only through the blood of Jesus Christ can we avoid the wrath of God.

---

[25] Calvin, *Commentaries*, 113.

Chapter 8 Discussion Questions

1. Why were King David's sins forgiven? Why were the sins of Nineveh forgiven?

2. What is regret? What is repentance? What is the difference?

3. Why was Jonah's mission in Nineveh successful? Was he responsible for the dramatic change?

4. The conversion of the pagan Ninevite king is nothing short of miraculous. What are similar conversions in the Bible?

5. What was the purpose of sackcloth and ashes?

6. Why did the king command that animals also fast and put on sackcloth?

7. Have you ever fasted? Was there a particular reason? If not, what held you back from fasting?

8. Do you think that modern society is more or less sinful than Nineveh? What are similarities between the two cultures?

9

Relenting

JONAH 3:10

When God saw what they did, how they turned from their evil way, God relented of the disaster that He had said He would do to them, and He did not do it.

THERE WERE TWO POTENTIAL OUTCOMES for Nineveh: God could destroy the city just as Jonah warned, or the citizens of Nineveh could repent, and God would spare the city. Verse 10 reveals that God did, indeed, spare Nineveh from destruction. The Bible never says Jonah's message included any indication of God's mercy, but mercy is what Nineveh received. The people of Nineveh were unfamiliar with the concept of God's redeeming love (hesed). According to Jonah 3:9, the Ninevite king had an inkling of God's mercy, "Who knows, God may turn and relent and turn from His fierce anger, so that we may not perish."[1] This God they had not previously worshiped

---

[1] The king unknowingly quoted Joel 2:13, "Return to the LORD your God, for He is gracious and merciful, slow to anger, and abounding in steadfast love; and He relents over disaster."

might show them mercy. They hoped that Jonah's message of impending doom was only a warning. The Ninevites must have had some semblance of hope since they were so repentant. Says Hugh Martin, "The absence of hope excludes the possibility of repentance."[2] If the Ninevites had no hope that God was gracious, merciful, slow to anger, abounding in steadfast love, and relenting from anger, they would not have repented. The Ninevite king may have had some understanding of who God was, but there was no reason to expect God to show mercy to a people who were not His. Therefore, when God relented from overthrowing the city, the hope of the Ninevite people was fulfilled and the entire population became acquainted with God's redeeming love.

God is not obligated to forgive us when we repent. God forgives us because He is gracious, merciful, slow to anger, abounding in steadfast love, and relenting from disaster. God longs to be merciful to us,[3] and He will. It's a powerful part of who He is. The Ninevites came to understand the power of God's mercy. The warnings in Scripture, such as in Jonah 3:4,[4] should not leave us inactive. They should serve to change our hearts based on God's mercy.

God did not relent from Nineveh's looming destruction because of outward rites, such as sackcloth and ashes, but on the renewing change that had occurred in the hearts of the Ninevites. The Ninevites obtained God's pardon through repentance and turning to God. God shows mercy when a nation is contrite. Once again, repentance prevailed over judgment. This certainly does not mean repentance earns salvation, because God requires a change of heart, and no one will seek His grace except he who hates his sins. The truth is that God relented from His destructive wrath over Nineveh's sins because of Jesus' sacrifice on the cross. God is timeless. Just as our justification looks back to Christ's death on the cross and its power to erase sin, God was able to apply Jesus' same cancellation of debt to Nineveh, even though Christ's crucifixion and resurrection were centuries in the future.

---

[2] Martin, 267.
[3] 2 Peter 3:9, "The LORD is not slow to fulfill His promise as some count slowness, but is patient toward you, not wishing that any should perish, but that all should reach repentance."
[4] Jonah 3:4, "Jonah began to go into the city, going a day's journey. And he called out, "Yet forty days, and Nineveh shall be overthrown!"

"The repentance of the Ninevites,[5] showed, at any rate, a susceptibility on the part of the heathen for the Word of God, and their willingness to turn and forsake their evil and ungodly ways."[6] Chrysostom said that the LORD did this "not only for two or three or twenty people, but also for a whole population, in the case of the great and marvelous city of the Ninevites, which had knelt and bowed its head over the pit of perdition and was expecting to suffer the blow from above."[7]

Does God Change His Mind?

In Jonah 3:4,[8] Jonah declared to the Ninevites, "Yet forty days, and Nineveh shall be overthrown!" And we know from Jonah 3:1[9] that this was the message that God told him to declare. So then, why was Nineveh not destroyed? Jonah's message never mentioned repentance or God's relenting of the destruction of Nineveh. It only ever mentioned destruction. Does this mean that God changed His mind? God is omniscient[10] and He knew that Jonah's message would spur the Ninevites to repent. If God knew He would spare Nineveh, did He send Jonah to deliver a deceptive message threatening destruction?

Another example where God seemed to change His mind is found in 1 Samuel 15:28-35.[11] In this account of King Saul and the Israelite army battling the Amalekites, the LORD commanded Saul to wipe out all of the Amalekites.

---

[5] Jonah and the other prophets of Israel and Judah had been preaching God's word to their fellow Israelites and Jews for centuries, and very rarely did the Israelites heed God's message. The Ninevites, on the other hand, put "hard-hearted Israel to shame." (J. Stek, "The Message of the Book of Jonah" *CTJ* 1969:4:23-50.)

[6] Keil and Delitzsch, 409.

[7] Chrysostom, 143.

[8] Jonah 3:4, "Jonah began to go into the city, going a day's journey. And he called out, "Yet forty days, and Nineveh shall be overthrown!"

[9] Jonah 3:1, "Arise, go to Nineveh, that great city, and call out against it the message that I tell you."

[10] Omniscient means that God knows everything: the past, the present, and the future.

[11] 1 Samuel 15:28-35 (NIV), "Samuel said to him, "The LORD has torn the kingdom of Israel from you today and has given it to one of your neighbors—to one better than you. He who is the Glory of Israel does not lie or change His mind; for He is not a human being, that He should change His mind." Saul replied, "I have sinned. But please honor me before the elders of my people and before Israel; come back with me, so that I may worship the LORD your God." So Samuel went back with Saul, and Saul worshiped the LORD. Then Samuel said, "Bring me Agag, king of the Amalekites." Agag came to him in chains. And he thought, "Surely the bitterness of death is past." But Samuel said, "As your sword has made women childless, so will your mother be childless among women." And Samuel put Agag to death before the LORD at Gilgal. Then Samuel left for Ramah, but Saul went up to his home in Gibeah of Saul. Until the day Samuel died, he did not go to see Saul again, though Samuel mourned for him. And the LORD regretted that He had made Saul king over Israel."

He specifically told Saul, "*Do not spare them*, but kill both man and woman, child and infant, ox and sheep, camel and donkey."[12] (italics added) Saul spared the Amalekite king, Agag, and the best of the livestock "to sacrifice to the LORD." God was angry with Saul for his disobedience and tore Saul's kingdom from him. 1 Samuel 15:29 tells us, "He who is the Glory of Israel does not lie or change His mind; for He is not a human being, that He should change His mind." But then verse 35 tells us that the LORD *regretted* that He had made Saul king over Israel.

Four different Scriptural truths support the idea that God does not change His mind:

1. God is unchangeable.[13] In Malachi 3:6,[14] God testifies "I, the LORD, do not change." James 1:17[15] says of the Father, "there is no variation or shadow due to change." Psalm 110:4[16] says, "the LORD has sworn and will not change His mind." We can trust that God cannot change any part of Himself, even His mind. When He makes promises and declares His will, we can rest peacefully in the knowledge that He will keep His word. While the world changes by the minute, God remains the same.

2. No force, good or evil, can make God change His mind. Ephesians 1:11[17] tells us that God "works all things according to the counsel of His will." "All things" refers to good and evil things. Nothing, not evil things nor the choices of men, can force God to change His mind. Scripture tells us that no one can thwart His plans. In Job 42:2, Job said to the LORD, "I know that you can do all things, and that *no purpose of yours can be thwarted*." (italics added) Isaiah 14:27 tells us, "For the LORD of hosts has purposed, and who will annul it? His hand is stretched out, and who

---

[12] 1 Samuel 15:3, "Now go and strike Amalek and devote to destruction all that they have. Do not spare them, but kill both man and woman, child and infant, ox and sheep, camel and donkey."

[13] Another way to say this is to say that God is immutable.

[14] Malachi 3:6, "For I the LORD do not change; therefore you, O children of Jacob, are not consumed."

[15] James 1:17, "Every good gift and every perfect gift is from above, coming down from the Father of lights, with whom there is no variation or shadow due to change."

[16] Psalm 110:4, "The LORD has sworn and will not change His mind, "You are a priest forever after the order of Melchizedek."

[17] Ephesians 1:11, "In Him we have obtained an inheritance, having been predestined according to the purpose of Him who works all things according to the counsel of His will."

will turn it back?" Nothing in the universe can force God to change His mind.
3. Since God is omniscient, He does not need to change His mind. Frequently, when we change our minds, it is because new information has become available. However, if God knows everything, there can be no new information. Therefore, He will not change His mind because of new information. Scripture tells us that God is "perfect in knowledge."[18] 1 John 3:20[19] says that "God knows everything."
4. Since God is perfect, He cannot change His mind. If God were to change His mind, it would imply that His previous thoughts or actions were mistakes. As God is perfect, He cannot make a mistake. Since God doesn't make mistakes, He doesn't change His mind. Romans 12:2[20] says that the will of God is "good and acceptable and perfect." Matthew 5:48[21] says "Our heavenly Father is perfect."

So, what about Jonah's prophecy of the destruction of Nineveh? Did God change His mind and decide not to destroy the city? No, because God is omniscient, He did not change His mind. Rather, the message that He gave to Jonah to proclaim to Nineveh was the catalyst necessary for the city to repent. Without Jonah's message of doom, the Ninevites would never have forsaken their sinful ways and turned to God. God knew that the Ninevites would repent. This did not come as a surprise to Him. Since it was God's will for Nineveh to repent, it was also God's will for God to relent from the prophesied destruction. Says Duguid, "Because God does not change, He is a consistently forgiving and merciful God, who always extends mercy to people who genuinely repent, which means that any threat of judgment in the Bible is always conditioned by the possibility of mercy."[22]

The Bible is clear that God can withhold mercy for objects destined for destruction.[23] God obviously planned to save the Ninevites from the wages of

---

[18] Job 37:16, "Do you know the balancing of the clouds, the wondrous works of Him who is *perfect in knowledge*." (italics added)
[19] 1 John 3:20, "for whenever our heart condemns us, God is greater than our heart, and *He knows everything.*" (italics added)
[20] Romans 12:2, "Do not be conformed to this world, but be transformed by the renewal of your mind, that by testing you may discern what is the will of God, what is good and acceptable and perfect."
[21] Matthew 5:48, "You therefore must be perfect, as your heavenly Father is perfect."
[22] Duguid, 50.
[23] Romans 9:14-18, "What shall we say then? Is there injustice on God's part? By no means!
[15] For He says to Moses, "I will have mercy on whom I have mercy, and I will have compassion

their sins. So why was it necessary to send Jonah at all? If there were 120,000 souls in Nineveh who did not know their right from their left, it is safe to assume they were unaware of the danger they were facing. If Jonah did not come and open their eyes to their looming cataclysm, they would not know they needed saving. God is jealous of our praise and thankfulness. Jonah prepared the ground of Nineveh's hearts to be fertile soil to reap an abundant crop of joyful praise and thankful love for God.

Second Chances
Our God is a God of second chances. Throughout the Bible, God gives people second chances. In the Book of Jonah alone, God gave three parties second chances: the sailors, Jonah, and the Ninevites. The sailors had led sinful lives; they had never worshiped the one true God. But those precious souls were allowed to repent and begin living for God in the stormy seas of judgment. Jonah was given the most obvious second chance in the book, and arguably in all of Scripture. Jonah blatantly disobeyed God when he attempted to flee to Tarshish. And yet, God restored him to the office of prophet and used him in a mighty way to save Nineveh. Before Jonah called out to the great city, the Ninevites were an evil, violent people. They were given a second chance to change their ways and repent before the LORD. In these instances, God forgave people, even when they did not love Him.

What about in the rest of Scripture? There were plenty of others who were also given second chances. During the plagues, Pharaoh was given ten chances to let God's people go. Sadly, even after those ten chances, he still changed his mind and tried to recapture Israel. King David, described as being "a man after God's own heart,"[24] sinned in a big way against God when he committed adultery with Bathsheba and then had her husband Uriah killed.[25] While God punished David, He gave him a second chance to continue as king.

---

on whom I have compassion." [16] So then it depends not on human will or exertion, but on God, who has mercy. [17] For the Scripture says to Pharaoh, "For this very purpose I have raised you up, that I might show my power in you, and that my name might be proclaimed in all the earth." [18] So then He has mercy on whomever He wills, and He hardens whomever He wills."
[24] 1 Samuel 13:14, "But now your kingdom shall not continue. The LORD has sought out *a man after His own heart,* and the LORD has commanded him to be prince over His people, because you have not kept what the LORD commanded you." (italics added)
[25] 2 Samuel 11.

The apostle Peter was given a second chance after he denied Jesus three times. Giving people second chances is what God does. It is a principal part of who He is. He loves His people and wants them to repent and turn to Him in faith.

Just as God has given His people in Scripture second chances, He does the same for us. When we sin against Him, He allows us to repent. He longs for us to repent and turn to Him, and when we do, He is there waiting to forgive us. Our God is "ready to be reconciled and is always prepared to embrace those who without pretense turn to Him."[26]

Why Forty Days?
In Jonah 3:4,[27] Jonah declared to the Ninevites, "Yet forty days, and Nineveh shall be overthrown!" Why did God give the Ninevites forty days? We know that God doesn't change His mind and that He is the same yesterday, today, and tomorrow. So why wait the forty days? In Genesis 2:15-17,[28] God commanded Adam not to eat of the tree of knowledge of good and evil. Should Adam decide to disobey God and eat of that tree, he would die. Not even a chapter later, Adam and Eve ate the forbidden fruit, but when they did so, they did not *immediately* die.[29] They stayed alive. Why didn't God kill them on the spot? 2 Peter 3:9 says, "The LORD is not slow to fulfill His promise as some count slowness, but is patient toward you, not wishing that any should perish, but that all should reach repentance." God was in no hurry to put Adam and Eve to death. He gave them time to repent from their sins and turn towards Him. It was the same way with Nineveh. God was patient with its inhabitants, giving them time to repent. And when they repented, He spared the great city. Isaiah 30:18 says, "The LORD waits to be gracious to you, and therefore He exalts Himself to show mercy to you. For the LORD is a God of justice; blessed are all those who wait for Him." Our LORD longs to be gracious and merciful to us.

Though the prophets failed to inspire repentance in Israel time after time, Nineveh didn't even need the forty days to repent. When we see our own

---

[26] Calvin, *Commentaries,* 113.
[27] Jonah 3:4, "Jonah began to go into the city, going a day's journey. And he called out, "Yet *forty days*, and Nineveh shall be overthrown!" (italics added)
[28] Genesis 2:15-17, "The LORD God took the man and put him in the garden of Eden to work it and keep it. And the LORD God commanded the man, saying, "You may surely eat of every tree of the garden, but of the tree of the knowledge of good and evil you shall not eat, for in the day that you eat of it you shall surely die."
[29] God did not lie or exaggerate the effects of eating from the Tree of the Knowledge of Good and Evil. Adam and Eve's sin brought death into a perfect world, and from that moment, their bodies began to slowly die.

country steeped in sin, should we shrug our shoulders and give up? Chronicles 7:14 says, "If my people who are called by my name humble themselves and pray and seek my face and turn from their wicked ways, then I will hear from heaven and will forgive their sin and heal their land." This is what we are to do! The author calls on believers to pray, seek God's face, and repent. This is precisely what occurred in Nineveh. We are in the exact same boat as Nineveh. God has given us time to repent. Chrysostom says it well, "After this, are we not ashamed? In only forty days, the Ninevites laid aside all their wickedness, but we, who have been urged and taught during so many days, have not gotten the better of one single sin."[30]

---

[30] Chrysostom, 143.

Chapter 9 Discussion Questions

1. Can you think of other instances in Scripture where God appeared to have changed His mind?

2. What are the four Scriptural truths that show us that God does not change His mind?

3. Who are some other people in the Bible that God gave second chances to?

4. Why do we not immediately die when we sin?

5. What are some examples of how God brings life from death?

6. Why do we hesitate to repent and turn to God in faith when we know that He will spare us His wrath?

7. What are some other Biblical examples of repentance prevailing over justice?

8. Is God's forgiveness based solely on man's repentance?

10

Resenting

JONAH 4:1-3

But it displeased Jonah exceedingly, and he was angry. ² And he prayed to the LORD and said, "O LORD, is not this what I said when I was yet in my country? That is why I made haste to flee to Tarshish; for I knew that you are a gracious God and merciful, slow to anger and abounding in steadfast love, and relenting from disaster. ³ Therefore now, O LORD, please take my life from me, for it is better for me to die than to live."

MY OLDEST SON CANNOT KEEP a secret for anything. If I want everyone to know something important, I tell him about it and ask him to keep it to himself. Within hours, the entire family will know. When he was 11, we attended a midnight release of a Harry Potter book along with his teenage sister. When we got home, he stayed up all night reading. At breakfast the next morning, he blurted out to his sister that one of the key characters died in the book. I thought she was going to kill him. I wasn't surprised at all. Of course he blabbed the biggest secret in the book. That's who he is. In our text for this chapter, the same thing happened with Jonah and God. Based on his knowledge of who God is, Jonah knew that God would forgive the Ninevites. But this was much more serious than the spoiled ending of a new book. Jonah was so angry that he said he wanted to die.

Nineveh's Repentance and Jonah's Nationalism

Many of us would love to be as effective at sharing God's Word as Jonah was in Nineveh. I get super excited when I share the gospel with someone and they step out in faith in Christ. Multiply that by 120,000, and I would be doing cartwheels. I'd be flipping out, bragging about the miraculous hand of God at work in the city of Nineveh.

But not Jonah. He resented the salvation of the Ninevites. Deep down, he still hated them. Despite the whole ordeal with the fish, despite being shown mercy himself, Jonah's heart had not changed. He still didn't like the Ninevites. Not one bit. This is not what we expected at all. We figured Jonah would be overjoyed at the salvation of 120,000 lost souls. But he wasn't.

While Nineveh's repentance was pleasing to God, it threatened Israel's national interests.[1] In relenting from Nineveh's destruction, God spared Israel's enemy just as He had spared Israel. How could God spare the very enemies of His chosen people? Instead of showing Assyria the kind of undeserving favor He granted to Israel, Jonah felt that God should have punished the Assyrians without giving them any chance to repent.[2]

> "Let us learn by the example of Jonah not to measure God's judgments by our own wisdom, but to wait until He turns darkness into light."
>
> *John Calvin*

When we consider Jonah's response, it seems out of proportion, but we must not discount how Jonah's nationalism affected him. In Jonah's eyes, God could show grace to His own people but no one else. Showing grace to Nineveh was just too much. Luther maintained that Jonah "was hostile to the

---

[1] Keller, 102.
[2] Stuart, 502.

city of Nineveh and still held a Jewish and carnal view of God."[3] Jonah's heart had not changed at all. Jonah was a part of God's chosen people and Nineveh was their greatest enemy. It is always easier to assume that God is on our side rather than our enemies. Perhaps a better question to ask than "Is God on our side?" is "Are we on God's side?" Hebrew nationalism remained the big idol in Jonah's life. It was this idol that justified Jonah's hatred of his fellow man. It was the idol that hindered him from rejoicing in the salvation of 120,000 lost souls.

It is easy to see that Jonah's pride about Israel's status as God's chosen people was a major idol in his life. What about us? What idols do we have in our lives that keep us from sharing the gospel with others? Are we, like Jonah, concerned about what our peers will think of us? Do we overly prioritize things like employment, recreation, education, pride in our country, school, theology, or denomination over God's command to share the gospel with others? Or worse, do we consider some people unworthy of God's grace and love? We are all "stubborn grace-resisters in our hearts, rebels not merely against God's justice and holiness but against His compassion and mercy as well."[4] We must align our priorities with God's if we are to share His message in this fallen world that so desperately needs to hear it.

Jonah's Prayer

An important thing to remember about the story of Jonah is that he didn't set out on a mission trip to bring Gentiles to a saving faith in God. Therefore, any joy brought about by the salvation of Nineveh was completely lost on Jonah.[5] Who can blame him? Jonah had to be exhausted. He'd lived quite the story in the previous few days: He ran from God, rode out a storm in a ship, and was tossed into the sea, where he was swallowed by a great fish and vomited up onto dry land. Jonah then had to walk 500 miles to Nineveh, where he preached God's judgment only to have God relent on promised destruction. Who can blame him for being in a foul mood? Jonah likely felt like this whole adventure was a waste of time. Jonah's exhaustion, I'm sure, played a role in his anger.

On a positive note, Jonah went directly to the One with whom he was upset. In Jonah 1, Jonah fled *from the* LORD. Now, in Jonah 4, Jonah flees *to*

---

[3] Keil and Delitzsch, 411-412.
[4] Duguid, 9.
[5] Timmer, 117.

the LORD. He didn't run or hide from God this time. Jonah is no enemy of God. Not by any stretch. He retained some seed of piety and obedience in his heart.[6] Rebellious though he may be, Jonah was still a child of God. He didn't keep his anger to himself. He wasn't silent. Instead, he prayed to God and wholeheartedly explained why he was upset. He approached the throne of God with all of his grief and rage and angst. Jonah felt comfortable enough in his relationship with God that he poured out his frustrations to God.

Jonah's Anger
In Jonah 3:9, God turned away from His anger. In Jonah 4:1, Jonah turned toward his anger. According to verse 2, Jonah was furious with God because God acted like God. Jonah's problem at this point was not Nineveh but the character of God. The Hebrew text in verse 1 expresses Jonah's anger as strongly as possible. The Hebrew word *hārāh* has two meanings. It usually means "to be angry," while other times, it means "to be hot." That's a great description of Jonah at this point of the story. Jonah is hot, physically, spiritually, and emotionally.

Jonah believed that for the Ninevites, there was a disconnect between God's justice and love. For him, they could not exist in the same place simultaneously. Additionally, Jonah was also very concerned about saving face with his fellow Israelites. They likely knew that he was to prophesy about Nineveh's destruction. If he returned to Israel and Nineveh remained, he would look like a false prophet. He had more regard for his reputation as a prophet than for the glory of God or the salvation of a city.[7]

Jonah's reaction to the sparing of Nineveh is similar to that of a petulant child who, when things aren't being done to his liking, pouts, takes his toys, and goes home. "Though Jonah hardly comes across as a hero anywhere in the book, he appears especially selfish, petty, temperamental, and even downright foolish in chapter 4."[8] Jonah, in the next two verses, justified why he fled to Tarshish. Just as I knew my son could not keep a secret about the Harry Potter book, Jonah knew that God was merciful and would forgive the Ninevites. He knew that God would relent and spare these enemies of Israel.

---

[6] Calvin, *Commentaries*, 119.
[7] Calvin, *Commentaries*, 120.
[8] Stuart, 502.

He knew these things, and yet he didn't want God to operate as God does. He wanted God to be jealous and judgmental rather than gracious and merciful.

Jonah based his anticipation of the sparing of Nineveh on what he knew about the character of God. In verse 2,[9] Jonah cites an ancient creed about Yahweh's grace. This creed lists five of God's attributes:
1. God was *gracious in* that He gave the Ninevites a new lease on life.
2. God was *merciful in* that He did not destroy Nineveh. Deep down, however, Jonah felt that mercy had to be deserved. He thought Israel deserved God's mercy rather than Nineveh.
3. God showed that *He was slow to anger* in that He gave the Ninevites 40 days to repent. While God was slow to anger, Jonah was not. Jonah may have felt that the immediate punishment of Nineveh was the only acceptable response to their sin. And yet, that is not what he had personally experienced in chapters 1 and 2. But when God didn't immediately punish Nineveh, Jonah melted down.
4. God was *abounding in steadfast love* toward the Ninevites. Throughout the Book of Jonah, God referred to Nineveh as "that great city." God loved the city of Nineveh.
5. By not destroying Nineveh, God *relented from disaster*. Perhaps Jonah would have been satisfied if God had merely delayed the disaster rather than relenting from it.

Just as he did in his prayer in Jonah 2, Jonah quoted God's Word back to Him. The attributes listed in Jonah 4:2 are the same ones listed in Exodus 34:6-7,[10] which reads, "The LORD passed before him and proclaimed, "The LORD, the LORD, a God merciful and gracious, slow to anger, and abounding in steadfast love and faithfulness, keeping steadfast love for thousands, forgiving iniquity and transgression and sin, but who will by no means clear the guilty, visiting the iniquity of the fathers on the children and the children's children, to the third and the fourth generation." What is particularly ironic is that Exodus 34:6-7 follows the worshiping of the golden calf at Mount Sinai. In that story, God spared the Israelites from certain destruction. In Jonah 4:2, God spared the Ninevites from certain destruction. These five characteristics of God are

---

[9] Jonah 4:2, "And he prayed to the LORD and said, "O LORD, is not this what I said when I was yet in my country? That is why I made haste to flee to Tarshish; for I knew that you are a gracious God and merciful, slow to anger and abounding in steadfast love, and relenting from disaster."

[10] And Joel 2:13, "Return to the LORD your God, for he is gracious and merciful, slow to anger, and abounding in steadfast love; and he relents over disaster."

the ones most frequently attributed to Him throughout the Bible. They are how God describes Himself. They are key to whom God is. The five attributes of God listed in verse 2 are called communicable attributes. That is, God and man can both have those attributes. However, none of those attributes describe Jonah. In fact, they describe what Jonah wasn't. And Jonah not only didn't appreciate those attributes, he seemed to view them as weaknesses of God.

The crux of Jonah's issue with God was that Jonah thought he knew better than God. He knew who should be saved and who shouldn't. He knew how things were supposed to run, while God did not. God was going to forgive those who didn't deserve it. And that was not how Jonah's God was supposed to act. It's easy to look back at Jonah's relationship with God and criticize Jonah. As Iain Duguid said, "All of this might be amusing if it weren't so close to home for us."[11] Don't we have our own standards that God must meet for Him to be God? Do we actually dare to stand in judgment when God acts the way He does? If you doubt this, keep in mind the frequency that both believers and non-believers question God's goodness when things don't go the way they want. We ask, "How can a loving God allow loved ones to get sick or die?" "How can a loving God allow natural disasters?" "How can a loving God withhold the blessing of children from a couple?" How arrogant! If you want to know what God thinks about us when we dare question His plans, consider His speech to Job in Job 38. God not only won the argument, but Job repented everything he said. We must humble ourselves, for we are getting too big for our own britches.

Jonah's Death Wish
In verse 3, Jonah told God it was "better for me to die than live!" Jonah was so fed up with God acting like God that he asked God to end his life. That's a pretty serious request based on flawed thinking. Was Jonah perhaps being a little overly-dramatic? Most people who contemplate suicide have experienced hopelessness. If Jonah's God was not going to act like Jonah expected, then Jonah could no longer hope in Him. But Jonah was basically telling God that He could forgive Israel's enemies "over Jonah's dead body!"

---

[11] Duguid, 62.

Jonah should have been the happiest man alive. He should have been walking on sunshine! His preaching helped save 120,000 people from physical and eternal death. Jonah had prophesied in Israel for years, and almost no one responded to his messages. Now, every single person responded. Let's compare Jonah's numbers in Nineveh to those of Billy Graham, arguably the greatest evangelist of modern times. It is estimated that the number of people Reverend Graham preached the gospel to at live events is 215 million. Of those 215 million people, 2.2 million responded to the invitations to become a Christian. Billy Graham, throughout his lifetime, had only a 1% success rate! While God used Reverend Graham to introduce 2.2 million people to Jesus, his success as an evangelist pales compared to Jonah. In Nineveh, 100% of the population repented. Every person from the least to the greatest, from the oldest to the youngest, from the lower classes to the nobility – everyone repented. Everyone! Jonah should have been more than happy with this wonderful miracle, but he wasn't. Jonah missed out on celebrating with God about the salvation of the Ninevites because he was so committed to his own idea of what they deserved.[12] Instead, he wished to die.

Jonah's cry out to God was the desperate plea of a man of God who had forgotten God's prior providence in his life. Wasn't Jonah the same prophet who declared in Jonah 2:9 that "Salvation comes from the LORD?" Had he forgotten that the salvation of the Ninevites came from the LORD? Jonah preferred death to serving a God who showed mercy to Israel's enemies. God treated the Ninevites better than He treated the golden-calf-worshiping Israelites at Mt. Sinai. To Nineveh, God had shown that He was gracious, merciful, slow to anger, abounding in steadfast love, and relenting from disaster. He judged Israel for the golden-calf worship by sending a plague[13] and had the Levites kill 3,000 Israelites[14].

Jonah just couldn't come to terms with the concept of salvation for the Gentiles. Interestingly, nowhere in the Old Testament does God say that He will withhold mercy and grace from Gentile nations. Jonah still hated the

---

[12] Duguid, 52-53.
[13] Exodus 32:35, "Then the LORD sent a plague on the people, because they made the calf, the one that Aaron made."
[14] Exodus 32:25-28, "And when Moses saw that the people had broken loose (for Aaron had let them break loose, to the derision of their enemies), then Moses stood in the gate of the camp and said, "Who is on the LORD's side? Come to me." And all the sons of Levi gathered around him. And he said to them, "Thus says the LORD God of Israel, 'Put your sword on your side each of you, and go to and fro from gate to gate throughout the camp, and each of you kill his brother and his companion and his neighbor.'" And the sons of Levi did according to the word of Moses. And that day about three thousand men of the people fell."

Ninevites. He did not want to see God be merciful to his enemies. Jonah hated "grace shown to those he thinks don't deserve it, especially non-Israelites."[15] But God is free to show mercy to whomever He chooses.[16]

Jonah was not the first person in Scripture to wish to die. Elijah experienced the same emotion. Both Jonah and Elijah wished to die when they felt that God had abandoned them. As you may recall, in 1 Kings 18, Elijah demonstrated God's power over the pagan god, Baal. Elijah came off this fantastic victory against the prophets of Baal and plunged into depression. Within a day or two, he said, "It is enough; now, O LORD, take away my life, for I am no better than my fathers."[17] Elijah wished for death because he was afraid that Israel's evil queen Jezebel would kill him. He was experiencing spiritual despair.[18]

Jonah, on the other hand, wanted to die because his prophecy about the destruction of Nineveh did not come true. Their reasons for desiring death were not the same. Elijah feared for his life. Jonah's reputation as a prophet had been tarnished. The apostle Paul also wished to die, although his reason was far different than Jonah's or Elijah's. Paul desired to die so that he might be with Christ.[19] However, he realized that he needed to stay in this world because of those to whom he was ministering. Paul's wish was a passing idea, while Elijah and Jonah were much more serious about their desire to die.

Closing Thoughts

It is easy to condemn Jonah for his biases. But aren't we all the same? "How often, are you and I like the elder brother on the return of the Prodigal Son in the story that Jesus told, standing outside the party with folded arms and tapping toes, resentful over the LORD'S grace to someone that we hate?"[20] We each have our own ideas of who God is and how He should act. We believe

---

[15] Timmer, 122.
[16] Romans 9:15, "For He says to Moses, "I will have mercy on whom I have mercy, and I will have compassion on whom I have compassion."
[17] 1 Kings 19:4
[18] Keil and Delitzsch, 411.
[19] Philippians 1:21-24, "For to me to live is Christ, and to die is gain. If I am to live in the flesh, that means fruitful labor for me. Yet which I shall choose I cannot tell. I am hard pressed between the two. My desire is to depart and be with Christ, for that is far better. But to remain in the flesh is more necessary on your account."
[20] Duguid, 53.

there are certain people that it is permissible for Him to forgive, but others should never be forgiven. We feel that certain sins are unforgivable. We feel that there are certain viewpoints so terrible that there is no way that God could ever forgive them. But that's not how God acts, does He? Our God is gracious and merciful, slow to anger, abounding in steadfast love, and relenting from disaster. Our God forgives the repentant. There is no sin too evil for God not to forgive. There is no person too far gone for God not to forgive. Repent of your ideas about how God should act. Repent of your self-righteousness over others. Ask God to show you His true nature and be open to understanding it.

There is freedom in believing in God's sovereignty over His creation. When we understand that God's ways are not like ours and trust Him explicitly, then we can have peace even in the face of overwhelming tragedy. We do not have to understand why something happens that seems horrible to our limited human thinking. We can trust that God is in control and He knows what He is doing. We don't have to figure it all out. Beginning with that trust, we can move on to extending His grace and mercy to others. And it is that response and winsome love and grace that will show others what is different about us. His love shining through us in the face of tragedy should be what sets us apart.

Chapter 10 Discussion Questions

1. Why was Jonah so upset over God's sparing of Nineveh?

2. What idols did Jonah have in his life that prevented him from sharing the gospel with others? What idols do you have in your life that keep you from sharing the gospel?

3. Do we have our own standards that God must meet for Him to be God? What are some of those?

4. What is Jonah's biggest issue with God? Why was Jonah so upset with Him?

5. What characteristics of God do you struggle with?

6. Was Jonah's desire to die justified? Is suicide ever justifiable? Why or why not?

7. In what ways was Jonah's attitude like that of the older brother in the story of the Prodigal Son? How are you like them?

8. Jesus addressed the question of God's grace and mercy being extended to Gentiles. Read the following passages and explain how the "crumbs" analogy applied to the salvation of Nineveh.

   • Matthew 15:22-28

   • Mark 7:25-30

11

God's Rebuke

JONAH 4:4-8

And the LORD said, "Do you do well to be angry?" ⁵ Jonah went out of the city and sat to the east of the city and made a booth for himself there. He sat under it in the shade, till he should see what would become of the city. ⁶ Now the LORD God appointed a plant and made it come up over Jonah, that it might be a shade over his head, to save him from his discomfort. So Jonah was exceedingly glad because of the plant. ⁷ But when dawn came up the next day, God appointed a worm that attacked the plant, so that it withered. ⁸ When the sun rose, God appointed a scorching east wind, and the sun beat down on the head of Jonah so that he was faint. And he asked that he might die and said, "It is better for me to die than to live."

MANY OF US STRUGGLE WITH anger. We get angry at the driver who cut us off. We get angry over our favorite team losing a championship game. We get angry when someone we love dies. While reasons to be angry vary from trivial to life-threatening, we have all experienced anger. Jonah was angry because he didn't think Nineveh deserved saving, but also because the salvation of Nineveh would make Jonah appear to be a false prophet. His reputation would crumble if his prophecies didn't come true. He cared more about what people thought about him than he did about the salvation of the Ninevites. Jonah 4:8[1] closes with Jonah asking God to take his life.

In the first part of Jonah 4, Jonah expressed his anger to God in prayer. God, in return, challenged Jonah, "Have you any right to be angry?" God is, in essence, asking Jonah, "Is it right for you to be angry that the same grace and mercy that were shown to you, were shown to someone else?" Desmond Alexander said that it is ironic that Jonah condemned God for not being angry at Nineveh. Yet, Jonah was being challenged regarding his own anger.[2] In verses 4-8, God rebuked Jonah in two ways: verbally and physically.

> Anger is an acid that can do more harm to the vessel
> in which it is stored than to anything on which it is poured.
>
> *Mark Twain*

God's Verbal Rebuke

God's rebuke began with asking Jonah, "Do you do well to be angry?" It was as if God said, "Hey Jonah, how's that anger thing working out for you?" The only one being hurt by Jonah's anger was Jonah. His anger had no bearing on God or the repentant Ninevites. There were so many things for Jonah to be glad about: God spared the lives of 120,000 people. Luke 15:8-10[3] tells us that angels rejoice when one sinner repents. They must have gone crazy when

---

[1] Jonah 4:8, "When the sun rose, God appointed a scorching east wind, and the sun beat down on the head of Jonah so that he was faint. And he asked that he might die and said, 'It is better for me to die than to live.'"

[2] Alexander, 127.

[3] Luke 15:8-10, "Or what woman, having ten silver coins, if she loses one coin, does not light a lamp and sweep the house and seek diligently until she finds it? And when she has found it, she calls together her friends and neighbors, saying, 'Rejoice with me, for I have found the coin that I had lost.' Just so, I tell you, *there is joy before the angels of God over one sinner who repents*." (italics added)

120,000 sinners repented! Jonah's ministry was beyond successful. Jonah should have been glad that God showed Himself merciful, gracious, slow to anger, abounding in steadfast love, and relenting from disaster. And yet, Jonah was so angry at God that he wished to die.

Rather than continue to witness to Nineveh, Jonah headed out of town to await its impending destruction. In Genesis 18:22-33, Abraham conversed with God about the looming destruction of Sodom and Gomorrah. Abraham bargained five times with God to spare Sodom, settling on God relenting of the promised destruction if ten righteous souls dwelled in the city. While Abraham had a vested interest[4] in God relenting from the destruction of Sodom, Jonah had no interest in saving the city of Nineveh. God wiped out Sodom since there were not even ten righteous people in the city. Nineveh, on the other hand, had over 120,000 repentant citizens, but rather than advocate for mercy as Abraham did, Jonah fully expected God to destroy it. He left the city in pouting silence and sat a safe distance away to watch the action. If Nineveh was going to be destroyed, Jonah wanted a front row seat.

However, Jonah had just lamented that he knew all along that God wouldn't carry out his terrible prophecy. So why sit in the desert and wait? Perhaps God's forty-day time limit was about to expire and Jonah wanted to see if God would change His mind. Despite reciting God's praise-worthy attributes of grace, mercy, and steadfast love just a few verses before, it appears that there was a disconnect between Jonah's head and his heart. He knew that God was a God of grace and mercy, but his actions show us that deep down, he didn't believe it with all of his heart.

> "Jesus is the prophet Jonah should have been. . . Jesus did not merely weep for us; He died for us. Jonah went outside the city, hoping to witness its condemnation, but Jesus Christ went outside the city to die on a cross to accomplish its salvation."
>
> *Tim Keller*

The Life and Death of a Plant
Since Jonah did not answer God's question about anger, God "appointed" an object lesson to further show Jonah the error of his thinking. The word "appointed" was used three times in these four verses. In verse 6, God

---

[4] Abraham's nephew Lot and his wife and daughters lived in Sodom.

appointed a plant to grow overhead to relieve Jonah from the hot sun. In verse 7, God appointed a worm[5] to kill the plant. Then, in verse 8, God appointed the east wind and scorching sun. The word appointed was used one other time in the Book of Jonah. In Jonah 1:17, God appointed the great fish to swallow Jonah. In each of these four instances, God displayed His power over nature and His providence to Jonah. God used each of these four appointments to bring Jonah back to Himself.

Jonah was hopeful that God was merely delaying the destruction of Nineveh and that God would relent from His divine mercy and ultimately wipe the city out entirely. Jonah built a booth,[6] or a small shelter, out of branches, grass, and leaves to the east of Nineveh to watch God repeat the destruction of Sodom and Gomorrah. Building his shelter on the eastern side of Nineveh was prudent as the wind blew from the east, and Jonah did not want to be downwind as God rained hellfire and brimstone down upon the city. Jonah obviously could not live in a city that was about to be destroyed, but living under the Middle Eastern sun was not a suitable alternative either. Jonah's tent was insufficient to protect him from the desert elements.

God had mercy on Jonah and provided a plant to give him shade. The plant displayed God's propensity to give, and the purpose of the plant was twofold: it kept Jonah from discomfort and it was intended to teach Jonah about God's grace and mercy. Jonah was glad about the plant. And yet, God's mercy was the very thing Jonah was upset with God about. When God displayed mercy to the Ninevites, Jonah got angry. However, when God showed mercy to Jonah by providing divine air conditioning, he was happy. In Jonah's mind, mercy was for God's chosen people only.

Jonah was exceedingly happy about the plant. At this point, the story of Jonah could come to a happy end. Nineveh and its fate no longer really mattered to him, and his disagreement with God was resolved. But God needed to continue with Jonah's object lesson. Just as Jonah was getting comfortable in the plant's shade, God appointed a worm to attack and kill the plant. God gave the plant its life. Therefore, He had the right to take it away. He gives and takes away. Job 1:21 says, "And he said, "Naked I came from

---

[5] God used a large animal – a huge fish – and a small animal – a worm – to bring about His sovereign will. Nothing in all of creation is exempt from His use.

[6] Booths are temporary. They are not permanent dwelling places.

my mother's womb, and naked shall I return. *The LORD gave, and the LORD has taken away* blessed be the name of the LORD." (italics added) That's the difference between Jonah and Job. At his lowest point, Job blessed the LORD. At what should have been his highest point, Jonah became angry with God over a wilted day-old weed. God had removed the shade which protected Jonah from the elements.

The Plant

There has been some discussion about what kind of plant it was. The Hebrew word used in verses 6,7,9 and 10 is *qiqayon,* which is translated simply as "plant." The Septuagint uses the Greek word *kisson,* which means ivy. The King James Bible identifies the plant as a gourd. Some hypothesize that the plant was a cucumber. It is unlikely that the plant was a gourd or a cucumber, as those plants require good soil and plenty of water. The ESV identifies the plant as *Ricinus Communis*, the castor oil plant. This makes sense, as the castor oil plant grows in sandy places, has broad leaves, and grows very quickly. However, it is easily killed by the slightest damage to its stem. Ultimately, though, all that matters about the plant is that God appointed it.

The Onslaught of the Elements

To make sure Jonah got the point, God appointed a fierce east wind to turn up the heat. Now, the east wind was not just a wind. Throughout the Old Testament,[7] the east wind was a symbol of God's judgment. Hosea 13:15, speaking about Israel, tells us, "Though he may flourish among his brothers, the east wind, the wind of the LORD, shall come, rising from the wilderness, and his fountain shall dry up; his spring shall be parched; it shall strip his treasury of every precious thing." In this verse, Hosea refers to the coming judgment of Israel, which would come from the east. That judgment would come in the form of the Assyrian army, dismantling the Northern Kingdom of Israel. Jeremiah 18:17 says, "Like the east wind I will scatter them before the enemy. I will show them my back, not my face, in the day of their calamity." Jeremiah refers to the east wind as the wind of storms, tempests, and parching heat. The east wind would deliver such things while God turned His back on Israel.

---

[7] The east wind appears in the Old Testament 17 times.

Perhaps the best-known reference to the east wind is found in Exodus 14:21. "Then Moses stretched out his hand over the sea, and the LORD drove the sea back by a strong east wind all night and made the sea dry land, and the waters were divided." In this incident, the east wind was used to part the Red Sea so that the Israelites might escape the Egyptian army. Once Israel had passed through the Red Sea, that same east wind closed the sea in judgment against the Egyptians. By having the east wind blow upon Jonah, God was sending his judgment in the form of unrelenting sun and heat.

Of course, if you are going to have an east wind, you should have the scorching desert sun to go with it. Jonah was literally being sandblasted, and the oppressive heat became too much for him. Verse 8 tells us that he became faint, likely experiencing sunstroke. The symptoms of sunstroke are physical weakness, mental anguish, and depression. This could explain Jonah's desire to die.

The fact that Nineveh was not destroyed shows that Jonah was both correct and incorrect. He was correct in knowing that God would relent and spare the city. He was incorrect because his prophecy that Nineveh would be destroyed in 40 days was ultimately wrong. Jonah was upset because his message, "In forty days, Nineveh will be destroyed." was proven untrue. Jonah's credibility had taken a hit. Deuteronomy 18[8] states that when a prophet has said something in God's name that didn't happen, that message was not from God. When Nineveh wasn't destroyed as promised, it seemed that Jonah's message was not from God. Jonah was more concerned about his own reputation than for the glory of God. Calvin says that "the cause of Jonah's grief was . . . that he was unwilling to be deemed a false or lying prophet."[9]

Jonah became excessively angry with God about the plant and the heat and repeated his death request, "Better for me to die than live." Jonah said he wanted to die, but God did not forsake him. God used four different means of providence to draw Jonah back, but Jonah wanted none of it. His heart grew

---

[8] Deuteronomy 18:21-22, "And if you say in your heart, 'How may we know the word that the LORD has not spoken?'— when a prophet speaks in the name of the LORD, if the word does not come to pass or come true, that is a word that the LORD has not spoken; the prophet has spoken it presumptuously. You need not be afraid of him."

[9] Calvin, *Commentaries,* 117.

harder. Jonah's emotions had overcome his heart and mind. We must be careful not to fall into the same trap. Calvin tells us to "learn how to repress in time our feelings and at the beginning to bridle them, lest if they should burst forth to a greater extent, we became at last altogether obstinate." [10]

Aren't we, like Jonah, more concerned about our own reputations than God's glory? As fallen beings, we tend to be more concerned about what others think of us than what God thinks of us. We have it all backward. The sad part is that it is easy to say that we don't care what others think, but the truth of the matter is that we do. This is perhaps most evident in churches today, where people act like they have it all together and tell each other that they are "fine" instead of being honest. Being honest with others about the troubles of life makes us feel weak and vulnerable. When we withhold these truths from the body of Christ, we miss the opportunity for the church to bear our burdens with us. We miss opportunities for God to work through the prayers and gifts of our Christian brothers and sisters. Bottling up our weaknesses and hiding from others is as old as Adam and Eve. Self-reliance seems laudable to our human minds, but the more we rely on ourselves, the less we rely on God.

Jonah would rather die than have his reputation tarnished. What about you? How do you respond when your reputation is at stake? Do you become anxious and try to hide the terrible things you have done? Do you exaggerate the positives and minimize the negatives? Why? Does what others ultimately think of you matter? Or does it only matter what God thinks? Our relationship with our Father is the only reputation we should be concerned about. The best way to become concerned about what God thinks is by spending time in His Word. For it is there that we understand how God thinks and acts.

---

[10] Calvin, *Commentaries,* 139.

Chapter 11 Discussion Questions

1. Did Jonah have the right to be angry?

2. When is anger righteous? Unrighteous? How do we decide?

3. Did Jonah's concern about his reputation influence his actions? If so, how?

4. Why did Jonah sit and wait in the desert? What does it tell us about his character?

5. Jonah knew about God's character (that God is gracious, merciful, slow to anger, abounding in steadfast love, and relenting from disaster), and yet he couldn't be sure God wouldn't destroy the city. Why do you think that is?

6. Strong emotions are part of being human. How could Jonah have taken his emotions to God instead of taking them out on God? What is the difference?

7. Have you ever focused on something as meaningless as a dead plant rather than on what was important? How can we change that?

8. Are you guilty of worrying more about what others think of you than what God thinks? How so?

12

God's Response

JONAH 4:9-11

But God said to Jonah, "Do you do well to be angry for the plant?" And he said, "Yes, I do well to be angry, angry enough to die." ¹⁰ And the LORD said, "You pity the plant, for which you did not labor, nor did you make it grow, which came into being in a night and perished in a night. ¹¹ And should not I pity Nineveh, that great city, in which there are more than 120,000 persons who do not know their right hand from their left, and also much cattle?"

IN VERSES 6-8, GOD PRESENTED Jonah with an object lesson, in which the point was to teach Jonah that salvation belongs to the LORD. Jonah's bold prayer at the end of Jonah 2[1] proclaimed the LORD's salvation and promised obedience. Yet here he is fainting away again and he has forgotten the wisdom he learned in the fish. And if he has forgotten the lesson he learned in the fish

---

[1] Jonah 2:7-9. "When my life was fainting away, I remembered the LORD, and my prayer came to you, into your holy temple. ⁸ Those who pay regard to vain idols forsake their hope of steadfast love. ⁹ But I with the voice of thanksgiving will sacrifice to you; what I have vowed I will pay. Salvation belongs to the LORD!"

already, a different type of lesson is called for. Why didn't God simply explain things to Jonah? That would have been much easier, but Jonah's track record of listening and obeying God was not great. He's at a 50% obedience rate. Therefore, God chose to use the object lesson of the castor oil plant and the worm. Object lessons are great in that they help simplify concepts and increase retention. The lesson of the plant and the worm is something that Jonah would not soon forget.

In the final three verses of chapter 4, God explained the object lesson to Jonah. God started by repeating His question, "Do you do well to be angry for the plant?" This time, Jonah answered God, but he repeated his request to die, "Yes, I do well to be angry, angry enough to die." Jonah was livid about a plant dying. A plant! Not something of lasting importance. Not something made in God's image! A plant! It wasn't even something Jonah planted or watered! If Jonah pitied a small plant that he did not invest in, how much more should he pity the city of Nineveh and its inhabitants, who were created in God's image? Jonah was upset about the plant, but his real problem was the hardening of his heart against the Ninevites.

In Jonah 4:10-11, Yahweh didn't simply scold Jonah for his petty behavior.[2] He confronted him about his anger about the plant and his rage against the Ninevites. Jonah's unfounded anger needed to be addressed. God began with the plant. He discussed how Jonah pitied the withered plant. Jonah had done nothing for this plant. He did not water it or tend to it; it grew because God appointed it to. Then God reminded Jonah that the plant was only a little thing. It grew and withered overnight. It was unimportant in the grand scheme of things. God then compared Nineveh to the plant. Nineveh, God told Jonah, was a great city with more than 120,000 people. Jonah did nothing to move the people's hearts so that they would repent. He delivered his prophecy of doom and left, unconcerned and unsympathetic to their plight. Any change of heart the Ninevites experienced was solely because of God. It was not Jonah's call to decide who lives and who dies. Creation and salvation belong to the LORD. "Just as God protected Jonah through the plant, He had shown the same protection to Nineveh through His compassion and grace."[3]

---

[2] Timmer, 130.
[3] Ferguson, 96.

As a result, Jonah had no right to be angry about the plant or the Ninevites. They were not his creation. They were both the work of God. Jonah's role in these instances was simply to obey God. That was all that was required of him. This time, he did obey, but he did so with an angry heart.

God's point was that Jonah's conduct toward the Ninevites was uncompassionate and inhuman. Like an angry teenager, Jonah didn't listen. He was angry at God about the plant and did not hesitate to tell Him so. If Jonah was angry enough to die because of this plant, should he not be just as compassionate toward these people? The truth was that Jonah cared more about a plant (and himself) than people.[4] The plant had been useful to him while the Ninevites were not. "Had Jonah not yet learned the lesson that the immortal souls of men are the most precious thing in the universe?"[5] There is nothing more important in all of life than the hearts and souls of men. And those hearts and souls should be set upon Christ alone.

The Ungrateful Servant

In Matthew 18:21-35,[6] Peter asked Jesus how often we should forgive. Jesus responded with the parable of the ungrateful servant. In the parable, a king had a servant who owed him a substantial amount of money. After the servant begged for forgiveness, the king canceled his debt. The servant, free from his debt, approached a fellow servant who owed him a small amount and demanded to be paid. When that man could not pay, the ungrateful servant

---

[4] Ferguson, 97.
[5] Ferguson, 83.
[6] Matthew 18:21-35, "Then Peter came up and said to Him, "LORD, how often will my brother sin against me, and I forgive him? As many as seven times?" Jesus said to him, "I do not say to you seven times, but seventy-seven times. "Therefore, the kingdom of heaven may be compared to a king who wished to settle accounts with his servants. When he began to settle, one was brought to him who owed him ten thousand talents. And since he could not pay, his master ordered him to be sold, with his wife and children and all that he had, and payment to be made. So, the servant fell on his knees, imploring him, '*Have patience with me, and I will pay you everything.*' And out of pity for him, the master of that servant released him and forgave him the debt. But when that same servant went out, he found one of his fellow servants who owed him a hundred denarii, and seizing him, he began to choke him, saying, 'Pay what you owe.' So, his fellow servant fell down and pleaded with him, '*Have patience with me, and I will pay you.*' He refused and went and put him in prison until he should pay the debt. When his fellow servants saw what had taken place, they were greatly distressed, and they went and reported to their master all that had taken place. Then his master summoned him and said to him, 'You wicked servant! I forgave you all that debt because you pleaded with me. And should not you have had mercy on your fellow servant, as I had mercy on you?' And in anger his master delivered him to the jailers, until he should pay all his debt. So also, my heavenly Father will do to every one of you, if you do not forgive your brother from your heart." (italics added)

had him thrown into prison even though he had pleaded for mercy the same way the ungrateful servant had pleaded with the king. When the king heard about the ungrateful servant's refusal to forgive, He recalled the debt and threw the ungrateful servant in prison until the debt was paid in full.

Jonah was very much the ungrateful servant. He had been forgiven much but was unwilling to forgive others. Other than being Israel's sworn enemy, the Ninevites never personally wronged Jonah. Their sins were against God. God had forgiven Jonah for disobeying Him, and yet Jonah refused to forgive the Ninevites for their sins against God. Jay Sklar says that "those who forget their experience with the forgiveness of God are the quickest ones to refuse to forgive others."[7] Jonah had already forgotten his experience of forgiveness in the fish. He had forgotten that salvation belongs to the LORD. God alone is responsible for salvation. He alone chose who would be saved. Jonah's responsibility was to obey God and call out against Nineveh, not to sit in judgment over them.

In the area of forgiveness, we, too, are no better than Jonah or the ungrateful servant. How much has God forgiven us but we are unwilling to forgive others, even when they repent? Without God's grace and mercy, we cannot make it through one minute of a day. Withholding grace and mercy from others is wrong. Since we have received God's grace and mercy, we are to freely give it to others. We must be willing to forgive one another. We must forgive much because we have been forgiven infinitely more.

Sharing the Gospel

For years, I believed that man, in his sinful state, could choose God. I used phrases like "choose Christ" or "made a decision for Christ." I loved watching the massive altar calls at Billy Graham crusades. However, upon studying the Book of Ephesians, I realized that mankind is dead in its sins.[8] A dead person cannot speak with others. A dead person cannot make decisions. Therefore, a dead person cannot "choose" to be saved. *They are dead.* They must have life

---

[7] Sklar, 420.
[8] Ephesians 2:1, "And you were dead in the trespasses and sins." Colossians 2:13," And you, who were dead in your trespasses and the uncircumcision of your flesh, God made alive together with Him, having forgiven us all our trespasses." Ephesians 2:5, "Even when we were dead in our trespasses, made us alive together with Christ—by grace you have been saved."

in them if they are going to do anything. The Holy Spirit must be at work in their hearts. Before He created the world, God decided who would receive the Holy Spirit and who would not. Salvation belongs to the LORD.

This "deciding" of God as to who will be saved is known as election. Election is defined as God's choosing of individuals who will receive His favor before they have done anything.[9] Rather than man "choosing God," election maintains that before the beginning of the world, God chose man.[10] Scriptural support for the doctrine of election can be found in Ephesians 1:3-5,[11] Romans 8:29-30.[12] 1 Thessalonians 1:4-5,[13] and 2 Thessalonians 2:13-14.[14]

In evangelism and all of life, the Holy Spirit goes before us and inhabits the hearts of those who will be saved. It is not our own doing. And yet, we are scared to tell others about Jesus. We shouldn't be. In predestining some to be saved, God has already done the work. We must pray that our work will yield results according to His will. While salvation belongs to the LORD, man's words are how He saves. We are His instruments and His mouthpiece, but we are not Him. God decides the destiny of His creation. Jonah repeatedly forgot this and his story is there to remind us not to do the same.

---

[9] Romans 9:10-13, "And not only so, but also when Rebekah had conceived children by one man, our forefather Isaac, though they were not yet born and had done nothing either good or bad—in order that God's purpose of election might continue, not because of works but because of Him who calls— she was told, "The older will serve the younger." As it is written, "Jacob I loved, but Esau I hated."

[10] John 15:16, "You did not choose me, but I chose you."

[11] Ephesians 1:3-5, "Blessed be the God and Father of our Lord Jesus Christ, who has blessed us in Christ with every spiritual blessing in the heavenly places, even as He chose us in Him before the foundation of the world, that we should be holy and blameless before Him. In love He predestined us for adoption to Himself as sons through Jesus Christ, according to the purpose of His will."

[12] Romans 8:29-30, "For those whom He foreknew He also predestined to be conformed to the image of His Son, in order that He might be the firstborn among many brothers. [30] And those whom He predestined He also called, and those whom He called He also justified, and those whom He justified He also glorified."

[13] 1 Thessalonians 1:4-5, "For we know, brothers loved by God, that He has chosen you, because our gospel came to you not only in word, but also in power and in the Holy Spirit and with full conviction. You know what kind of men we proved to be among you for your sake."

[14] 2 Thessalonians 2:13-14, "But we ought always to give thanks to God for you, brothers beloved by the LORD, because God chose you as the firstfruits to be saved, through sanctification by the Spirit and belief in the truth. To this He called you through our gospel, so that you may obtain the glory of our Lord Jesus Christ."

And Also Much Cattle

Jonah ends rather abruptly with God asking Jonah the question, "And should not I pity Nineveh, that great city, in which there are more than 120,000 persons who do not know their right hand from their left and also much cattle?"

The reader is not privy to Jonah's response, if any, to God. By leaving us hanging, the reader is urged to self-examine and reflect upon the story of Jonah.[15] What is important is not how Jonah responded to the divine object lesson but how you and I respond to it today. Do we truly believe that salvation belongs to the LORD? How does this affect our daily lives? It's one thing to know that salvation belongs to God; it's another thing to live it.

The fact that salvation belongs to God should greatly relieve us. We do not have to earn our salvation. That responsibility belonged to Jesus Christ, and He has already taken care of it. Because of His sacrifice on the cross, we do not have to worry about being good enough to get to heaven. Rather, we obey God's law, not out of obligation, but out of love for the One who has forgiven us through His grace and mercy.

We must question ourselves, "Is there any way that I am like Jonah, unreconciled to the will of God – His will in His Word?"[16] Horace, in Satires 1.1.69, says, "Why are you laughing? If the name is changed, the story told is about you." As much as we don't like to admit it, we are all like Jonah, even though we shouldn't be. We unlovingly serve a loving God. We are, like Jonah, self-centered, not others-centered. Jonah's priority was Jonah. Our priority is ourselves. We need to rearrange our priorities. In Matthew 22,[17] Jesus explained our priorities when He summarized the law. Our first priority is to love God with all of our being. Our next priority is to love our neighbor as we love ourselves. Jonah did neither. He did not love God with all his being, or he would never have fled from God. He did not love his neighbors,

---

[15] Timmer, 133.
[16] Martin, 358.
[17] Matthew 22:36-40, "Teacher, which is the great commandment in the Law?" And He said to him, "You shall love the LORD your God with all your heart and with all your soul and with all your mind. This is the great and first commandment. And a second is like it: You shall love your neighbor as yourself. On these two commandments depend all the Law and the Prophets."

the Ninevites, as much as he loved himself or he would not have callously wished for their destruction and eternal damnation.

We must be sure not to emulate Jonah in our interactions with others. We are to show mercy and grace, even to our enemies. We must be slow to anger, even when we have every right to be upset. We are to be full of God's redeeming love, sharing it with those who need it. To be unmerciful is a grave disservice to the One who has shown us great mercy.

What about the final four words, "and also much cattle?" Why was this brought up? First, God had every right to spare Nineveh if only because of the cattle. Secondly, even though Jonah did not care about the Ninevites, perhaps, as God suggested, he might have compassion for their herds.[18] If Jonah was able to grieve over a dead plant, he might grieve even more over countless livestock. Humans are often still like this. We may be moved by a tear-jerking ad for the ASPCA to end the suffering of innocent animals but turn a blind eye to the suffering of our fellow man.[19]

Where are They Now?
The story of Jonah leaves us hanging. We are left with so many questions. Since the book ends so abruptly, people often ask about Jonah. What happened to him? What about Nineveh? Did the repentance last at all? What about the fish? What happened to it?

Ultimately, we don't know what became of Jonah. According to one extra-biblical source,[20] God restored Jonah to his family. According to Josephus, "when he [Jonah] had published [God's message to Nineveh], he returned home."[21] Other traditions have Jonah's wife meeting him in Jerusalem upon his return from Nineveh. Some traditions have him entering paradise without dying. It is highly unlikely that Jonah returned to Israel and continued in his calling as a prophet since his prophecy regarding Nineveh had not been fulfilled. The bottom line is that we don't know what became of God's holy runaway.

What about Nineveh? What happened to the repentant Ninevites? Sadly, their repentance did not last. After all, it takes only one generation to turn away from the LORD. Within a generation or two, Jonah's worst fears became

---

[18] Alexander, 131.
[19] People have no problem with movies and television showing people die, often in gruesome ways. But the protests abound if entertainment shows a dog dying.
[20] 3 Maccabees 6:8, "And you, Father, looked upon Jonah, when he was wasting away in the belly of a sea monster from the depths, and you restored him unharmed to all his family."
[21] Josephus. *Jewish Antiquities,* 9.10.2.

reality. Assyria, under the leadership of Shalmaneser V, defeated the Israelite king, Hezekiah in 722 B.C. The northern ten tribes of Israel and its capital city, Samaria, fell to the Assyrians. Approximately 27,000 Hebrews were exiled to the cities of the Medes and Babylonians.[22] In return, conquered peoples from other parts of the Assyrian empire were relocated to Israel. Over time, the Hebrews who remained in Israel intermarried with these other people, and their offspring became the Samaritans of the New Testament.

The Book of Nahum speaks directly to the destruction of Nineveh. In just three short chapters, Nahum prophesied against Nineveh. While most of his prophecies were general,[23] Nahum did make some very specific predictions about the city's fall. The city of Nineveh fell in 612 B.C. to the Babylonians. This fulfilled the prophet Nahum's prediction that God would completely destroy the city.[24] Nahum 1:8[25] states that Nineveh would be flooded, resulting in her destruction. During the siege of Nineveh, there was a breach of Nineveh's wall along the Tigris River, which flooded the once great city and allowed the Babylonians to plunder and destroy it. In Nahum 1:9[26] and 1:15,[27] we are told that the city would not rise up again. This was fulfilled by the fact that Nineveh, since its fall, was never rebuilt. To this day, the city lies in ruins. In fact, it wasn't until 1846 that the ruins of Nineveh were discovered. Nahum 2:13[28] and 3:15[29] speak of a fire in Nineveh. The burning of captured

---

[22] Younger, K. Lawson (1998). "The Deportations of the Israelites". *Journal of Biblical Literature*. 117 (2): 201–227.

[23] General prophecies pertain to any city under attack. For example, Nahum 2:10 says, "Desolate! Desolation and ruin! Hearts melt and knees tremble; anguish is in all loins; all faces grow pale!" That could be said about any city under siege.

[24] Nahum 1:12, "Thus says the LORD, "Though they are at full strength and many, they will be cut down and pass away."

[25] Nahum 1:8, "But with an overflowing flood He will make a complete end of the adversaries and will pursue His enemies into darkness."

[26] Nahum 1:9, "What do you plot against the LORD? He will make a complete end; *trouble will not rise up a second time*." (italics added)

[27] Nahum 1:15, "Behold, upon the mountains, the feet of him who brings good news, who publishes peace! Keep your feasts, O Judah; fulfill your vows, for *never again shall the worthless pass through you; he is utterly cut off*." (italics added)

[28] Nahum 2:13, "Behold, I am against you, declares the LORD of hosts, and I will burn your chariots in smoke, and the sword shall devour your young lions. I will cut off your prey from the earth, and the voice of your messengers shall no longer be heard."

[29] Nahum 3:15, "There will the fire devour you; the sword will cut you off. It will devour you like the locust. Multiply yourselves like the locust; multiply like the grasshopper!"

cities was a common practice of the Babylonian army. They employed a "scorched earth" policy in which nothing was left behind. Additionally, archaeological research has revealed evidence that Nineveh was burned. By 605, the Assyrian Empire was gone, and another empire was on the rise: Babylon.

The city of Nineveh, despite being one of the largest cities in the world during Jonah's time, declined in size until the Middle Ages, when it became uninhabited. Mosul, the city across the Tigris River from Nineveh, began to grow as Nineveh's population dwindled. By the 1200s, Nineveh was mostly abandoned. The ruins of Nineveh lie across the Tigris River from Mosul. Over the years, Assyrian artifacts have been excavated from the ruins of Nineveh and are now housed in museums around the world.

Interestingly, Assyrians today are predominantly Christian. Most of the Assyrian population is Catholic, Syriac Orthodox, Eastern Orthodox, or Protestant. Today, most Assyrians live in Syria or the United States.

So what about the fish? What happened to it? The great fish swam peacefully throughout the Mediterranean Sea for the rest of its life. However, having developed a taste for man, a descendant of the great fish was rumored to have terrorized a small New England town in 1975.[30]

---

[30] https://www.imdb.com/title/tt0073195/

Chapter 12 Discussion Questions

1. Why does the Book of Jonah end with God's question unanswered?

2. Did Jonah's prophecy about Nineveh come true?

3. Why do you suppose God destroyed Nineveh, never to return?

4. The Book of Jonah is included with the prophetic books and yet it contains almost no prophecy. Why?

5. Why did God use an object lesson to teach Jonah? What was the point of the object lesson?

6. Do you believe that salvation belongs to the LORD? How does this affect our daily lives?

7. What are some common objections to the doctrine of election? How would you respond to those?

8. Have you ever acted like the ungrateful servant? Quick to be forgiven, but slow to forgive?

PLEASE REVIEW

You have reached the awkward part of the book where I ask you to leave me a review on Amazon, Google, or Goodreads. Believe me, I hate this as much as you do. However, I am swallowing my pride and asking anyway. Please! Whether you loved or hated it, you have made it this far, so please leave a review. Here's the thing: reviews play a big role in determining whether or not someone will read my book. Leaving a review will help me out a lot. If you liked this study, please recommend it to others. Oh, and thanks for reading my book. It means the world to me.

I can't stand typos. If you are like me, you can't either. Typos are like gremlins. No matter how many times a book has been edited, they magically appear. So, if you see a typo I missed, please email me at timothyjmulder@gmail.com.

Also, if you'd like to reach out to me, please write me at the above email address. I'd love to know what you think!

Thanks!

More by Timothy J. Mulder

Suffering in Silence: Ministering to Those With Mental Illness

Mental illness affects millions of Americans. Often, those afflicted will develop substance abuse problems or will die from suicide. Surely, there must be something the church can do to help. The author considers questions such as: Why are those who suffer from mental illness so often misunderstood? What are common misconceptions about mental illness in the church? How are churches and other ministries well positioned to help people struggling with mental illness? How can you best minister to those with mental illness? Join the author as he explores how to better understand mental illness, so you may better minister to those who suffer from it.

Ruth: A Story of God's Redeeming Love

The Book of Ruth is one of the most famous short stories of all time. In just four chapters, the reader is exposed to faithlessness, death, unwavering integrity, and redemption. Ruth provides an intimate view into the back story of the lineage of King David. Set in the time of the Judges, when "everyone did what was right in their own eyes," the wholesomeness and honesty of Ruth are a welcome breath of fresh air. In this study, we cover such topics as God's loving-kindness, the foreshadowing of Christ, waiting on God's timing the providence of God, and the redemption of Naomi. Join the author as he takes an in-depth, Reformed look into one of the greatest redemption stories of all time.

The Armchair Theologian's Guide to the Westminster Confession of Faith

Do you ever feel as though you have read your Bible but wish you could better explain what you believe? Do you wonder how the Bible applies to our world today? Are you frustrated when confronted with viewpoints that are not Scriptural, but struggle to disprove them? The Westminster Confession of Faith is a topical arrangement of the Bible into doctrinal truths. It was written to organize the Bible into a unifying summary of what Christians believe and to combat heresy. The Westminster Confession of Faith is as relevant today as when it was written nearly 400 years ago.

This book goes through the WCF in a user-friendly format, which includes the traditional and modern English versions of the WCF. It also highlights and counters unbiblical doctrine and creates talking points perfect for explaining Scripture to young believers or for cozy armchair discussions with friends.

What's Wrong With the Chosen?

The Chosen is arguably the most well-received religious television series ever. It has received rave reviews, including a 9.8 out of 10 rating at IMDB. According to the show's producers, over 108 million people have watched since December 2022. It has been translated into over 50 languages and has multiple Bible studies based on its content. With such widespread support, what could be wrong with it?

Is *The Chosen* Biblically accurate? Does it matter? A poll of reformed pastors and teachers showed that 87% are concerned about unbiblical content and consider the show a threat to uninformed believers. *What's Wrong With The Chosen* provides a Biblical critique of the show. The author's four objections to *The Chosen* are discussed, followed by an in-depth analysis in which every scene in seasons 1-3 are evaluated for historical and Biblical accuracy.

The Despicable Dozen – Bad Guys of the Bible

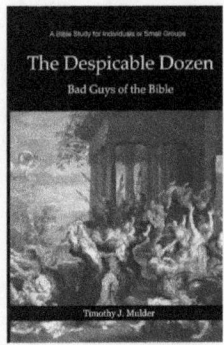

Browse any Christian bookseller, and you will see plenty of Bible studies on the heroes of the faith. What about the terrible, evil people in the Scriptures? God's inerrant Word includes these villains for a reason. Why are there no Bible studies about them? We know that God uses the "good guys" and the "bad guys" of the Bible to accomplish His perfect will. This study looks at the baddest of the bad: the despicable dozen.

The twelve villains in this study include those guilty of heinous sins, while others are included because of *whom* they sinned against. Our study will examine liars, adulterers, traitors, murderers, corrupt politicians, human traffickers, and despots guilty of murder and infanticide on an unfathomable scale. Upon finishing this study, you should better understand the sovereignty of God: His ability to use good and evil to accomplish His perfect, eternal plan.

www.ingramcontent.com/pod-product-compliance
Lightning Source LLC
LaVergne TN
LVHW011912080426
835508LV00007BA/487